PRESSURE
BASKETBALL

JACK RAMSAY

Director of Athletics
Head Basketball Coach
St. Joseph's College

Prentice-Hall, Inc.

PRESSURE
BASKETBALL

Englewood Cliffs, N.J.

Pressure Basketball, by Jack Ramsay
© 1963 by Prentice-Hall, Inc., Englewood Cliffs, N.J.

Library of Congress Catalog Card Number: 63-12272

PRINTED IN THE UNITED STATES OF AMERICA

69910—BC

To my wife

Jean,

> *a constant source of inspiration*
> *and*

"The Little Five,"

> *who are capable of dispelling*
> *even the gloom of defeat*

Acknowledgments

The author gratefully acknowledges the assistance rendered by the following in the preparation of this book: photographer *Louis P. Tucker,* secretary *Eileen White,* illustrator *Thomas Lynam,* assistant coach *Jack McKinney,* equipment manager *Dennis Flanagan,* personal advisor *Reverend Harry B. Degnan,* and *the players* from St. Joseph's College, LaSalle College, St. Charles Seminary, and Philadelphia College of Textiles and Science who were the patient subjects for the picture sequences used.

Preface

Before one undertakes the job of coaching an athletic team, it is essential to determine the objectives which he will seek for his team, each player, and himself. He must not only consider the objectives, but how he is to attain them. Once these objectives have been set, the coach must never deviate from them unless he is convinced that some alteration is necessary for the over-all well-being of those concerned with his team. This will be his philosophy of coaching.

A COACHING PHILOSOPHY

These objectives probably will be idealistic. There will be times when, in retrospect, the coach will realize that he has not attained the objectives he set for himself, his players, and his team. However, he must continue to strive for them since they represent the goals which he feels are vital for the participants to pursue on and off the playing field—at the moment and in later life. The coach must aim high and work hard to achieve his objectives. He must endeavor to have his players accept them. He does this knowing there are great benefits to be derived by each participant who earnestly seeks the goals, even though they are not attained.

Application of the philosophy. The philosophy will contain the principles by which the coach functions. It will influence every aspect of his endeavor. It will include the guideposts regulating his conduct and the conduct of his players. It will determine his team's style of play, the tactical methods he employs in the game, and even the way he conducts practice. The coach's philosophy will influence his relationships with the administration and faculty members of his school. It will reach into his relationships with family and friends, with spectators, with members of the press, and all others with whom he associates. Such a philosophy is required of every coach regardless of his sport.

NATURE OF THE GAME

The game of basketball, however, is rather unique by its very nature and seems to require a particular kind of philosophy. Basketball, more than any other sport, requires for success a careful blending of individual talents into precision team play. Such team play must emerge from a frantic, rapidly changing environment, in which the tempo of play is often at fever pitch for the entire game. Basketball is a game which demands a specially conditioned athlete—one capable of top-speed performance for extended periods. It is a game which requires tremendous physical endurance as well as speed, coordination, and an ability to adapt readily to constantly changing conditions. Basketball requires certain personal traits. Characteristics such as cooperation, self-sacrifice, self-discipline, loyalty, poise, and determination are sought in the players.

A game which demands so much has commensurate benefits to bestow on the sincere participant. It remains for the coach to assure the delegation of maximum benefits to those in his charge.

BASKETBALL AT ST. JOSEPH'S

St. Joseph's College has had an exciting tradition of basketball success. Under the inspirational guidance of William (Bill) Ferguson, who coached from 1927 to 1952, a basketball philosophy emerged over the years which might be summed up in one word—HUSTLE! The basic principle of this philosophy was that each player expend a maximum effort every second he was on the court. Although a relatively small school, St. Joseph's College has faced top national competition for decades and managed to come away with more than its share of victories.

Personal considerations. During my tenure as head basketball coach, which began in the 1955-56 season, I have attempted to carry on this philosophy and tradition. By playing against top competition, at home and away, with a predominantly local player squad, a great challenge is presented to the individual player and to the team. The arduous task of preparing for the season, the frequent role of underdog, and the realization that only through a determined, all-out effort will victory come within grasp—all help to make basketball an experience with great application for later life.

Our immediate objective is to develop a winning team and a feeling of pride in this accomplishment by each squad member. This objective is sought, not for the mere sake of winning—although we feel that this is certainly important—but also because of the lessons which it imparts as an aspect of our American culture and our democratic way of life. We want our boys to be able to stride into the game of life with the same firm purpose with which they enter a game of basketball. We hope they will be poised, well-equipped, and confident of winning the battle. We feel that basketball has helped scores of former players do just that.

Style of play. The style of play which we have adopted at St. Joseph's is compatible with the basic principles of the philosophy mentioned. It stresses hustle and determination. Since these characteristics are inconsistent with a passive style of play, we want every phase of our game to be aggressive and explosive. We have found that the great majority of our players enjoy this style and have taken pride in their accomplishments. This approach to basketball coaching is described in succeeding chapters.

Table of Contents

Preface • *vi*

    A COACHING PHILOSOPHY   *vi*
    NATURE OF THE GAME   *vii*
    BASKETBALL AT ST. JOSEPH'S   *vii*

Part I. The Development of Defense • *1*

  1. The Role of Defense • *3*

  2. Individual Defense • *7*

    THE MECHANICS OF DEFENSE   *7*
    BASIC MAN-TO-MAN PRINCIPLES   *11*
    SPECIAL SKILLS   *15*
    4 DRILLS FOR INDIVIDUAL DEFENSIVE DEVELOPMENT   *24*
        Coaching Tips   *26*

  3. Man-to-Man Team Defense • *29*

    10 PRINCIPLES OF DEFENSIVE TEAM PLAY   *30*
        Coaching Tips   *46*

  4. The Zone Press • *47*

    THE 3-1-1 ZONE PRESS   *48*
    THE 2-1-1 ZONE PRESS   *60*
    THE 1-2-2 ZONE PRESS   *65*
        Coaching Tips   *69*

5. Adjustment of Available Material to the Pressing Defense • *71*

FULL-COURT MAN-TO-MAN PRESS   *72*
HALF-COURT MAN-TO-MAN PRESS   *73*
THE ZONE PRESS   *74*
    Coaching Tips   76

6. Strategic Use of the Pressing Defense • *79*

    Coaching Tips   82

7. The Standard Zone Defenses • *85*

1-2-2 ZONE   *86*
    Coaching Tips on the 1-2-2 Zone   89
1-3-1 ZONE DEFENSE   *89*
    Coaching Tips on the 1-3-1 Zone   92
TEACHING THE ZONE DEFENSE   *92*
    Coaching Tips on General Use of Zone Defense   93

8. Defensive Practice Sessions • *95*

PRE-SEASON PRACTICE   *96*
DAILY SCHEDULE   *97*
GAME PRACTICE   *100*
    Coaching Tips   102

Part II. The Development of Offense • *103*

9. Relationship of Offense to Defense • *105*

    Coaching Tips   108

10. Individual Offensive Development • *109*

BALL HANDLING   *110*
SHOOTING   *123*
FOUL SHOOTING   *135*
    Coaching Tips on Free Throw Shooting   138
13 DRILLS ON OFFENSIVE FUNDAMENTALS   *139*
    Coaching Tips   148

11. Team Offense • *151*

THREE-LANE FAST BREAK *151*
 Coaching Tips on the Fast Break *154*
ST. JOSEPH'S MULTIPLE MAN-TO-MAN OFFENSE *155*
LOW POST ATTACK *162*
 Coaching Tips for Man-to-Man Offense *163*
 Coaching Tips for Zone Offense *166*

12. Situation Offenses • *167*

 Coaching Tips on Attacking the Pressing Defense *170*
FREEZE OFFENSE *171*
ZONE FREEZE *174*
 Coaching Tips on the Freeze Offense *174*

13. Special Considerations • *175*

THE JUMP BALL SITUATION *175*
 Coaching Tips on Jump Ball Situations *179*
 Coaching Tips on Out-of-Bounds Plays *184*

Part III. The Season • *185*

14. Training the Team • *187*

ISOMETRIC EXERCISES *192*

15. Game Preparation • *197*

16. Coaching the Game • *203*

THE STARTING LINEUP *203*
THE OPPONENT *205*
YOUR TEAM *207*
INDIVIDUALS *207*
SUBSTITUTING *208*
THE TIME-OUT *210*
HALF TIME *212*
END OF THE GAME *212*

17. Tournament Play • *215*

TOURNAMENT PRACTICE *215*

18. Post-Game Relationships • *219*

Index • *225*

PART 1

The Development
of Defense

CHAPTER 1

The Role
of Defense

Relationship of defense to philosophy. A basketball team's style of play must be predicated upon the defensive system which it employs. It has always seemed incongruous to me that a coach would adopt a particular style of offensive play before full consideration was given to the defense to be used. However, it seems that many coaches spend most of their time planning their offense and attach only incidental significance to the vital defensive phase of the game.

Promoting "defensive thinking." At St. Joseph's we feel that defense is the foundation and heart of our game. It is primarily through the medium of defense that we manifest the hustle and aggressiveness expressed in our philosophy. We try to promote a positive defensive attitude among our players. We want them to feel that our kind of defense will win games for us. We want our players to take pride in their ability to accomplish our defensive objectives. In order to accomplish them, we strive to develop each player so that he is basically sound, aggressive, challenging and daring in his defensive play.

The offensive aspect of defense. We strive to make our offense a natural outgrowth of our defense. We must be alert to shift quickly from defense to offense in order to take advantage of steals and deflected and intercepted passes. We try to obtain as many such easy field goals as possible. Since this success depends upon defensive skill, we devote the greatest amount of pre-season practice time (about 65 percent) to the fundamental individual and team tactics demanded by our defensive principles.

Types of defense. The defense referred to is fundamentally a *pressing man-to-man.* It is an aggressive attack on the opponent. It demands an adamant defensive attitude and a tremendous all-out effort by each player. It requires careful attention to the defensive fundamentals of stance and movement. The pressure defense makes use of the overplay, jump switches, double-ups, and an element of risk in order to obtain possession of the ball.

We will frequently resort to the *zone press* to realize our objectives. This variation blends well with the man-to-man style in the "pressure cooker" and produces a savory type of game which whets the basketball appetites of player, coach, and spectator.

A third ingredient in our defensive recipe is the *standard zone defense.* We turn to this formation occasionally in order to keep our opponent off balance.

With these defensive forces prepared, we feel we are ready to begin each new season.

General objectives. We have two general objectives in the pressing defenses we employ:

1. Prevent the opponent from playing the kind of game he wants to play.

2. Maintain constant pressure on the opponent to force him into ill-timed maneuvers on which we might capitalize.

Let us examine briefly each of these objectives. We attempt to force our opponent into a different style of play because we feel that he will operate less efficiently in a style less familiar to him. Therefore, if our opponent uses a set play offense, we try to prevent him from getting his plays started. If our opponent runs a pattern style of offense, our objective is to disrupt the pattern so that it is never completed. If he concentrates on working off a post (high, deep, or side), we attempt to keep the ball away from that objective. If the opponent is a slow and deliberate team, we try to speed up the tempo of play by forcing action through defensive pressure. If it is a fast-breaking team, we want to slow him down by pressuring the rebounders and overplaying the outlet pass receivers.

The second objective helps us to attain the first. In a sense, it implements the first because, by exerting pressure on our opponent, we force him to play a different kind of game than he planned. Beyond this factor is, of course, the desire to capitalize on the results of pressuring (steals, interceptions, opponent's violations) to stimulate our offensive attack.

Our general defensive objectives, therefore, touch both the defensive and offensive phases of the game. The pressure may be applied over the full-court, three-quarter court, or half-court. It may even take place at the conventional defensive position at the top of the circle. It may be a man-to-man or zone press.

Regardless of the type press to be utilized, or at what point on the court it is applied, we strive to force our opponent from his predetermined plan of attack and, at the same time, get our own offense off to an explosive start.

CHAPTER 2

The development of team defense is dependent upon the skillful execution of basic individual maneuvers. We devote a great many hours to individual defensive practice, stressing proper position, form, and movement.

THE MECHANICS OF DEFENSE

Defensive stance and position. The defensive stance of the player is of the utmost importance. In playing the man with the ball, we favor the fundamental position as pictured in *Figure 1a.* You will note that the player's knees are flexed, and the foot and hand (palm upward to flick up at the ball) nearer an imaginary basket-to-basket court division are extended. The back is fairly straight, and the head is up, with eyes riveted on the mid-section of the man with the ball. Attention is fastened on this area because it is the offensive player's least effective faking medium. He may fake with the ball, his shoulders, feet, head or arms, but when his mid-section moves, the defender can be certain that there is no fake involved. It also allows the defender to "see" a wide area from this central point through the use of his peripheral vision. The remaining hand is extended downward and away from the defender to help protect against the base-line drive and bounce pass.

7

Fig. 1a: **Defensive Stance**

Fig. 1b

Fig. 1c

In playing the man without the ball, the same basic position is maintained except that the defender turns more toward the ball—the degree of turn dependent upon the distance of his man from the ball. The defender should be able to include both the ball and his man within his vision. In *Figure 1b* the man without the ball is close enough to receive the next pass. Consequently, he is played tightly. In *Figure 1c* the defender playing the man at side-court turns more toward the ball, and loosens a few steps in that direction. We find that this stance best enables the players to adopt the rules of operation which are stated below.

Coaches at clinics often ask why we assume this particular foot stance. We take this position for two reasons:

1. It is the best position for overplaying the man without the ball. This is true because the defensive man can see both the ball and the man he is playing from the overplay position. He cannot do this with the other foot extended.
2. The defender playing the man with the ball is so placed that his weakest side offers him the most help from his teammates.

We do not force the man with the ball to either the middle or sideline as a matter of policy. I feel the weak side of the defensive man playing the ball is the side of the extended foot. If the extended foot is nearer the basket-to-basket court divider, then the defender is going to be strongest where he has the least help (the baseline) and weakest where he will receive the most help (the middle). Actually our objective is to prevent the man with the ball from advancing in either direction. We realize, however, that we won't always be able to accomplish this. Therefore, if a driver succeeds in beating our defensive man, we prefer that this player goes to the middle rather than to the baseline. Our basic position and stance assist us in making this defensive move.

If, therefore, his man has the ball, the defender assumes a stance as described, his extended foot aligned with the crotch of his opponent. He plays this man tight enough to prevent the good shot *or pass.* He is also ready to move (using the glide step) with this player if he drives in either direction and will endeavor to halt his advance by maintaining body position between him and the basket.

If the offensive player does not have the ball, the defender forces him away from the player in possession by maintaining a strong overplay position. His immediate objective is to prevent his man from receiving the pass; or secondly, to at least force his man away from his desired position in order to receive the ball.

An exception to the principle of foot stance occurs when one is playing a man without the ball on the same side of the court as the man *with* the ball. In this situation the defender plays with the foot nearest the ball-holder extended. In this position, he is able to overplay more vigorously.

Defensive movement. Concerning defensive movement, we encourage our players, when at all practicable, to use the boxer's glide step or "defensive shuffle." This movement is a rapid "step, close, step" maneuver in which the defender maintains the stance described above

Fig. 2a

Fig. 2d

Fig. 2b

Fig. 2e

Fig. 2c

Fig. 2f

Fig. 2, a-f: Pressure on the Dribbler

and does not cross his feet. This movement is made with the weight *slightly* forward on the balls of the feet and evenly distributed between the front and rear feet. This distribution permits the player to move in any direction—forward, rear, or lateral—with equal facility. If the defender moves to protect against a drive in either direction, the first move is in the direction of the offensive player with the corresponding foot. For instance, if the drive is in the direction of the extended foot, the defender drops that foot quickly and then slides (step, close, step) with the offensive move—maintaining body position between the driver and the basket. If the drive is toward the rear foot, the defender drops that foot further, then slides to check that movement. Forward defensive moves are accomplished in the same manner. The man with the ball is approached with a quick shuffle step, weight well balanced—allowing the defender to move effectively with the drive in either direction.

Although we attempt to perfect this skill through practice, we realize that there will be times when the defensive man is going to have to turn and run with his opponent. Therefore, we require him to maintain position using the "shuffle" as long as he is able to check his opponent. If his opponent begins to gain an advantage (with or without the ball), the defensive man must run with him until he has checked this advantage. Then he returns to the shuffle. (*See Figure 2, page 10.*) In this series the defensive man (No. 4), has checked the dribbler's progress with the shuffle (*2 a,b,c*), runs with the dribbler as he starts to gain an advantage (*2d*), shuffles again (*2e*), then tightens up on the man after the dribbler has been stopped (*2f*). Persistent practice will greatly improve the defender's ability to check his opponent's progress by the shuffle technique.

Basic Man-to-Man Principles

Once the players have acquired a reasonable degree of form and skill in stance and movement, we stress the individual rules of operation. One set of rules governs the situation for playing the man with the ball; another for playing the man without the ball.

Playing the man with the ball

1. Halt the advance of the man with the ball. Force him away from his objective.
2. Maintain pressure on the man until he gets rid of the ball.
3. Prevent man from taking a good shot.
4. Force him into a "bad pass position."

It is imperative for the defender to be able to stop the dribbler. This is the most vital aspect of the pressing defense. If the defensive players (most often the back-court men) can accomplish this task, it immediately puts the offensive team under pressure. The man with the ball must make a play. If we stop him in the back-court, he also has a time factor with which to be concerned.

We often pick out areas on the court where we want the dribbler stopped. The strategic reasoning behind the decision on where to pick up the opponent is discussed more completely in Chapter 6, "Strategic Use of the Pressing Defense." It is sufficient here to say that the opponent's general ball handling ability, possible height advantage, physical condition, depth in reserves, mode of offensive attack, and the game situation are considered in making this defensive move.

Checking the advance of the dribbler is a task which requires constant practice and dogged determination. However, it can be done. It *must* be done to play the pressure defensive game. Inability to realize this objective results in a loosely played, porous defense which is accessible by a variety of attacks. Players must be impressed with the necessity of this fundamental tenet of pressure defense.

Once the defender has succeeded in stopping the dribbler, he should maintain pressure on his opponent—moving up on him with arms active, so that a good shot *or pass* is impossible. The defender must also be prepared to retreat quickly if his opponent passes to a teammate and cuts for the return pass. (This sequence is illustrated in *Figure 3*.)

Again we see the defender challenge the dribbler (*3 a,b*). As the pass is made (*3c*), the defender uses his body position to check his man's first move, then loosens quickly and maintains position between his man and the ball (*3 d,e*). This is an important move for the defensive man to make. It takes concentrated practice to prevent the cutter from freeing himself and receiving the return pass.

Fig. 3, a-e:
Checking the Cutter

Fig. 3a

Fig. 3b

Fig. 3c

Fig. 3d

Fig. 3e

Playing the man without the ball

1. Maintain position *between the man and the ball.* Force him away from his objective.
2. Keep the ball in sight at all times.
3. Challenge the opponent's reception of all passes.
4. Be alert to intercept or deflect any pass which the defender feels he has a good chance of getting a hand on.

5. Be alert to pick up any open cutter or dribbler if he is advancing into scoring territory.

The first rule will sound like heresy to the more traditional coaches. It is vital to the pressure game, however. It is by this tactic that the passing outlets are closed off. Without this principle, our premise calling for pressure on the man with the ball would be seriously weakened. We would become vulnerable to the give-and-go attack, since the man with the ball can usually get a pass to an unchallenged teammate regardless of the efforts of a single defender. If the tightly played passer has an easy outlet, he has much greater freedom to cut and receive the return pass. However, if we stop the progress of the man with the ball, then close off the passing outlets, we are in an excellent position to capitalize on our opponent's hurried, and often misdirected play.

We like to play all positions in this manner, including the high post. However, we are usually a bit more conservative in playing the high post when meeting the opponent at half-court than when we press him at full-court. When defending at half-court, we will play the post-man hard on the ball side, ready to move out after any pass in his direction. If the post-man is stationary, we play in front of him even when picking up at mid-court.

The high post-man is always played from the front when pressing full- or three-quarter court. When playing from the front, the defender faces the ball and relies on his feel, an occasional glance, and the actions of the man with the ball for awareness of the post-man's location. Lob passes are challenged by the post defensive man and the weak side defensive forwards.

Rebounding. The aggressive, challenging defense demands special rebounding tactics for the individual player. While these tactics are illustrated and discussed more fully in the succeeding chapter, it is well to mention the basic responsibilities here.

Although the burden of rugged defensive rebounding falls on the larger players, each man has responsibilities in this important phase of the game. The fundamental move required of all players is blocking their opponents off the board. Because of his over-playing position, the defender must adjust quickly to block-out position when the opponent shoots the ball. This must be an aggressive act by which the defender moves *to* contact position *inside* (toward the basket) his man and holds this position, countering the efforts of his opponent to go to the board. Care must be exercised so that the defender does not move *into* the offensive player. He moves to contact position and holds that position, establishing a broad base with feet apart, knees flexed and elbows out in preparation for his leap for the ball.

The player holds his position until he sees the direction of the rebound, then he pursues the ball if he thinks he can obtain possession. If the errant shot bounces away from the individual, he maintains his position until he has determined that his teammate has possession.

The effort for possession is a leaping, spread-eagle thrust in which the player grasps the ball in a vise-like grip and turns ready to initiate the offensive play. *Figure 20* (*see page 43*) illustrates the proper technique for these moves. *Diagram 49* (*see page 148*) shows a drill that can be used to establish good defensive and offensive rebounding habits.

SPECIAL SKILLS

We require the fundamental performance described above of all personnel. However, the success of our defense depends in part upon the skill of key personnel—especially the back-court men—to steal the ball from their opponents and to properly effect two-on-one defensive blitzes by which we are able to obtain possession of the ball. Although some players are naturally endowed with "quick hands," which enable them to steal more readily than others, persistent practice toward this objective will enable the less skilled players to awaken unrealized talents. Some of the best ball-stealers I have coached have been boys who lacked exceptional speed, but who acquired a keen sense of anticipation and practiced hard to exploit their legerdemain.

Defensive fake. One of the techniques utilized by these specialists is the *defensive fake.* This maneuver, which resembles the fencer's parry and thrust in body movement, is especially disconcerting to dribblers lacking in poise and confidence. Even the skilled ball-handler has been known to suffer at the hands of the defender who occasionally varies his fake with an all-out thrust for the ball. *Figure 4* illustrates this particular tactic. The defender (No. 24) has faked a thrust for the ball (*4a*), then retreats using the defensive shuffle (*4 b,c*). Noting that the dribbler is keeping the ball high, the defender goes for the ball (*4d*) and flicks it

Fig. 4a   Fig. 4, a-f: **Defensive Fake (man with ball)**   Fig. 4b

Fig. 4c   Fig. 4d

Fig. 4e   Fig. 4f

away (*4e*) just before the dribbler was able to change direction. Now in possession and a clear floor ahead, No. 24 drives for the basket.

The "defensive fake" may also be applied when playing the man without the ball. Proper technique may lure the passer into attempting a play which the faking defensive man has anticipated. *Figure 5* illustrates such a maneuver. The side-court defensive man is overplaying his man (*5a*) and fakes a step out toward the approaching dribbler as if to double-up (*5b*). The passer, seeing his open teammate cut toward the basket, starts his pass in that direction (*5c*). The defensive man quickly retreats, however, and intercepts this pass (*5d*). The other defensive teammates are ready to help out if needed. (*See Fig. 5 on page 17.*)

Of course, this defensive move must be exercised with care. If the defensive man lunges out each time the ball moves in his direction, his offensive man will certainly "backdoor" him, *i.e.*, cut behind the defensive man toward the basket to receive a scoring pass. However, if the defender

Fig. 5, a-d: **Defensive Fake (man without ball)**

Fig. 5a

Fig. 5b

Fig. 5c

Fig. 5d

varies this move with an occasional double-up and a hard, straight over-play of his man, the defensive fake can be very profitable.

Double-up. We refer to the two-on-one defensive maneuver as the *"double-up."* Although we have no definite rules on when to utilize this tactic from our man-to-man defense, we spend a great deal of time working on situations in practice so that players will recognize a "good risk" opportunity. Generally speaking, we feel it is a good risk to attempt the double-up if:

1. the second defender can approach the man with the ball while the latter's back is turned;
2. there is a close lateral hand-off;
3. the offensive player with the ball is driving blindly into the second defender's position.

Fig. 6a   Fig. 6, a-f: **Double-Up (blind side)**   Fig. 6b

Fig. 6c   Fig. 6d

Figure 6 illustrates the first condition. *Figure 6a* shows both defenders tight on their men, but as the dribbler starts laterally across court
(*6b*), the second defender (No. 24) loosens and edges toward the ball
(*6c*). With the dribbler still moving away from his man, No. 24 moves up
and effects the double-up with No. 4 (*6 d,e,f*).

Figure 7 illustrates the second condition for a possible double-up—
when there is a close lateral handoff. No. 11 starts his dribble toward his

Fig. 7, a-e:
Double-Up (lateral move)

Fig. 7a

Fig. 7b

Fig. 7c   Fig. 7d   Fig. 7e

teammate as both defensive men check hard (*7 a,b,c*). As No. 11 hands off and goes through, both defenders jump out on the man with the ball (*7d*) and effect the double-up (*7e*). With other teammates on the floor, much of the risk is eliminated from this maneuver. The team aspects of the double-up are treated in the following chapter.

The third condition for the possible double-up is shown in *Figure 8* (*see page 21*). The sequence shows the standard "guard around" play. The guard has passed to the forward and moves to receive the hand-off (*8a*). The defensive forward has loosened slightly in anticipation of the hand-off. (Note third defensive man in play.) As the guard receives the hand-off, the double-up is made (*8b*). The weak side guard (No. 24) has come in to check off a return pass to the cutter (*8c*).

Although we urge our players to be alert for these situations, we feel it is important that each individual discover for himself the limits of his ability. Haphazard chasing for double-ups can be disastrous against a smart ball-handling team.

This tactic requires a great deal of practice. The immediate objective of the double-up is not to steal the ball. Of course, if the man in possession carelessly hangs the ball out for the defender, we want our players to flick at the ball in an effort to effect a quick steal. On most occasions, however, we are trying to force the man in possession into a bad passing position so that one of the other three defenders may intercept the errant pass. Care must be exercised so that defensive men do not foul the offensive players. They should maintain a close position, wedge him into the trough of a "V," and harass him with rapid arm and leg movements. Players engaged in the double-up follow the plane of the ball with corresponding arm movements. Some coaches advocate the use of both arms in this tactic, keeping them rather close together, following the path of the ball. This technique is advisable if the defender is able to do this with-

20

Fig. 8, a-c: **Double-Up**
(side post driver)

Fig. 8a

Fig. 8b

Fig. 8c

out reaching across the offensive player and without losing his balance. (*See Figure 6f, page 19.*)

Defensive flick. Another technique we have found valuable in obtaining ball possession is the "defensive flick." This is a tactic whereby the defensive man taps the ball away from behind the dribbler. While some-

21

what risky, it has proved itself very productive for the skilled practitioner. The theory behind this move is that if the defender can tap the ball from behind the dribbler to one of his teammates, this player is then free to receive a pass with a clear floor ahead.

Figure 9 (*see page 22*) illustrates the technique of flicking the ball away from the dribbler in a one-on-one situation. The guard has over-

Fig. 9, a-e: **Flick from Behind (one-on-one)**

Fig. 9a

Fig. 9b

Fig. 9c

Fig. 9d

Fig. 9e

played the dribbler to such an extent (*9a*) that he forces him to spin with the dribble and turn his back to the defensive man (*9b*). As the dribbler turns, the guard follows his movements (*9c*), then reaches through to flick the ball (*9d*). With his defensive teammates playing between their men and the ball, the guard is reasonably certain that one of them will obtain possession (*9e*). This leaves the front-court open for his cut to the basket.

A second opportunity for this move arises from a situation similar to that favorable to the "double-up." This occurs when the dribbler has turned his back on the defense. (*See Figure 10.*) In this sequence, defensive man No. 24 notices the dribbler's lack of awareness after a lateral hand-off in the back-court (*10 a,b*). Leaving his man after the defensive switch has been made (*10c*), the guard manages to get a piece of the ball and flick it into a pocket flanked by his teammates (*10d*). Note defensive man No. 34 moving out in the sequence to protect the play against a return pass to No. 11. Once assured of possession (*10e*), No. 24 breaks for his basket to receive a lead pass and the easy field goal.

Fig. 10, a-e: **Flick from Behind (four-on-four)**

Fig. 10a

Fig. 10b

Fig. 10c

Fig. 10d   Fig. 10e

This tactic must also be used with discretion. Players must be made aware of "good risk" opportunities. As has been stated regarding the "double-up," haphazard attempts to steal will only result in a porous defense which yields easy field goals. Conversely, proper application of this and the other "special skills" will produce a devastating defense—tough to play against, exciting to watch, and a pleasure to coach.

4 DRILLS FOR INDIVIDUAL DEFENSIVE DEVELOPMENT

(1) Group drill stressing proper form and movement. (*Figure 11*). The squad is lined up at a double arm interval so that there is ample freedom of movement. After players have been checked for proper stance, the team captain (or other member) leads the team in the defensive

Fig. 11 **Group Shuffle**

shuffle—side to side, forward and back. The squad follows the leader wherever he moves. This is a good morale drill as well as an excellent conditioner. The length of time spent in this drill is increased as stamina and skill in movement are acquired. Begin with a one-minute drill and build from that.

(2) **One-on-one hands behind back drill.** (*Figure 12*). This drill (*see below*) is used to emphasize the practice of maintaining body position while defensing the dribbler. The coach matches players according to speed and ball-handling ability. Players will surprise themselves at their ability to check the dribbler. The dribbler's lateral movement is limited from side line to foul lane. The offensive player attempts to go the length of the court for the field goal.

Fig. 12, a-f: **Individual Shuffle**

Fig. 12a   *Fig. 12b*   *Fig. 12c*

Fig. 12d   *Fig. 12e*   *Fig. 12f*

(3) One-on-one drill. This drill allows full use of all the defender's faculties. Encourage the use of defensive fake, thrust for steal, proper body position, and defensive movement in checking the advance of the dribbler. This drill is used full-court, half-court, and at the traditional position at the top of the circle (*Diagram 1*).

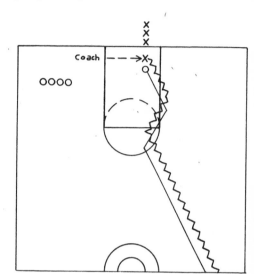

Diagram No. 1

(4) Two-on-two full-court drill. This drill affords great practice in switching and doubling-up, as well as in individual fundamentals. It also helps to develop defensive teamplay. (*Figures 6* and *15 on pages 18 and 36* illustrate the kind of play that can be developed in this drill.)

COACHING TIPS

1. "Sell" your players on the importance of defense. Locker room slogans, watchwords, pictures will help you do this.
2. Be meticulous in demanding proper stance and movement during pre-season practice sessions. If the habit becomes firmly set then, you won't have to worry about this during the season.
3. Use group and individual drills to build individual defensive skills and stamina.
4. Emphasize the vital importance of tough individual defensive play.
5. Emphasize the importance of each player restricting the offensive movement of his opponent.

6. Encourage players to maintain an awareness of the position of the ball—even though it may cost the team an occasional field goal.

7. Encourage the defensive player to take "good risks" in his efforts to obtain possession of the ball.

8. Keep a record of the number of "steals" made by each man and post this along with shooting percentages, rebounding figures, and other offensive facets of the game.

CHAPTER 3

Man-to-Man
Team
Defense

General objectives. Once the individual players have acquired a reasonable degree of competence with the fundamentals of defensive play, the next objective is to incorporate these individual skills into a team defense. The objectives called for on a team basis flow from those which were stressed individually. The over-all objective as a team is to force our opponent into a type of game at which he operates at less than maximum efficiency. The further we force him to depart from the offensive objectives which he seeks, the more likely we are to win the game.

Necessity of team play. The pressing defense is necessarily a team defense. By that I mean that unless there is harmonious team play among all five defensive players, the results can be disastrous. On the other hand if there is a high degree of team play the results will be gratifying to the coach, to the players, and exciting to the spectator.

Rules of operation. If we put into practice the rules of operation mentioned in Chapter 2, "Individual Defense," we are going to have a pressure type game as a team. It will be a kind of defense which gives the offensive team no breathing space. This defense will force them into

29

difficult situations time and again from which the defensive team will be able to gain possession before the offensive team has had a good opportunity to score. In order for this style of defense to operate efficiently, there are certain rules of operation which must be adopted by the team as well as by the individual player. We have developed a set of principles for such team defensive play. It is important that each player be cognizant not only of his individual responsibilities but also of his team responsibilities. While these two are interdependent, team success hinges heavily on the group application of these principles.

10 PRINCIPLES OF DEFENSIVE TEAM PLAY

1. Maintain a defensive stance, knees flexed, head up; foot nearer vertical court division forward; hands in close while moving; forward hand up on man with ball; eyes on midsection of opponent with ball.

2. Overplay near or next potential pass receiver.

3. Use peripheral vision to see both man and ball—but especially the *ball.*

4. Never turn your back on the ball. Face the ball, keep the lanes jammed by backing through as offensive man moves without the ball.

5. Use defensive shuffle in defensive movements; rely on the position of body to impede offensive moves. Don't cross feet in movements.

6. Slough off men without ball (except the next potential pass receivers), look for pass interception, pick up driver or pass receiver, or draw charge from offensive player; *keep position between man and ball.*

7. "Jump switch" on all lateral back-court offensive movements involving the ball; "hedge" on vertical moves involving the ball, using defensive fake.

8. Defensive man playing screener has option of doubling-up on ball when it seems a sound risk.

9. If defender has given up his man in an attempt to steal and has failed, he must be quick to pick up the open man in recovering.

10. Concentrate individual defensive efforts around the position of the ball; strive to get possession at every opportunity.

Fig. 13, a-c:

Team Pressure Position

Fig. 13a

Fig. 13b

Fig. 13c

A brief explanation is required for full understanding of these principles. Let us analyze each of these principles and point out the factors which are important for efficient application to the team situation.

Rule No. 1–Stance and movement: As we have indicated in "Individual Defense," we spend a great deal of time working on the maintenance of the proper defensive stance. Illustrations in Figure 1 show what this stance is. We strive to have each player maintain this stance all the time the opponent has the ball. *Figure 13* illustrates the position we like to have our players achieve as a team. Note the over-play by the next potential pass receivers in *13a*. No. 3 passes to his side-court teammate, who is forced to come out quite high to receive the pass (*13b*). Weak side men drop off and still remain between their men and the ball. In *13c*, the ball is on its way to the high post. The front defenders drop in on that position while the weak side defensive forward slides almost under the basket. This defensive action keeps constant pressure on the offensive team. Such pressure is possible because of proper stance and movement by the individuals.

Rule No. 2–Overplay the next or near potential pass receiver: This takes practice in recognizing which of the offensive players falls into this category. This is especially true, of course, if the opponent utilizes a moving offense wherein there is a rapid interchange of position by the players. With concentration, defensive players will recognize when their men become potential pass receivers. This position *must be challenged at all times.* The reception of a pass by this player must be placed in great jeopardy. (Refer again to *Figure 13*).

Rule No. 3–Awareness of position of the ball: We readily realize that not all players have the same degree of peripheral vision. We have had some players who had a great sense of knowing where the ball was at all times and were still able to check the position of their opponent. This, of course, is the ideal—when the defender can "see" both the man he is playing and the ball even though there is not direct vision toward either. As a general rule of thumb, we tell our players to fix their eyes approximately midway between the ball and their man. Most players find this rule enables them to keep both the ball and their men within the "fringe" area of their vision, which is what we want.

For the majority of players, however, this skill is somewhat limited. In contrast to the traditional defensive axiom, "stay between your man and the basket," we prefer that the defender be more conscious of the position of the ball than his man. This *does not* mean that we advocate a defense which permits individual offensive players to cut freely while defenders stand watching the ball. It *does* mean that if we are going to play a pressure game as a team, each player has a responsibility to know the position of the ball at all times and is ready to move quickly to break up any offensive threat.

Rule No. 4–Facing the ball: We feel that, in keeping with the principles which have already been stated, there should never be a time when the defender turns his back on the ball. This applies even if the offensive man gives and goes or cuts behind the defender without the ball. In this

Fig. 14, a-e: **Forward Draws Charge**

Fig. 14a

Fig. 14b

Fig. 14c

Fig. 14d   Fig. 14e

situation, we prefer that our defensive men face the ball and move in the general direction of the cutter, rather than face-guard their opponents. We have illustrated this move previously in *Figure 3*. We feel this is a reasonably safe principle and that the times we have been hurt by its application have been few in number compared to the occasions whereby we have obtained possession of the ball.

Our emphasis in stressing Rule No. 5—use of the glide step, or what we refer to as the defensive shuffle, for team movement—has been strengthened by a realization that players can, after sufficient practice, stay with their men by concentrating on a quick shuffle and by maintaining defensive position. Proper application of this move is basic to the success of individual and team defense.

Rule No. 6–Slough off the man without the ball: This is vital to the success of this team defense. Practice is required to know when to overplay and when to slough off. We have referred to the overplay in principle No. 2. It is just as important to know when to slough off and to leave one's man in an attempt to pick up a free cutter or dribbler. This is when team play is vitally important.

In *Figure 14* we see a series in which the side-court defensive man moves out to pick up the loose cutter. The offensive player coming toward the dribbler (*14a*), noting the overplaying position of his defender, starts his cut to the basket (*14b*). The man with the ball starts his pass as the weak side defensive man moves into position to close the gap (*14c*). Defensive man No. 40 gets into position as No. 4 hustles to cover the open deep man (*14d*). The play ends as No. 40 draws the offensive charge of No. 11 (*14e*). It is possible, if this player (No. 40) anticipates quickly enough, even to intercept the pass in a play of this kind.

Another application of this principle is practiced by weak side defensive men. In *Figure 14 f,g,h* (*see page 35*), the weak side forward lends assistance to his teammate whose man has driven past him (*14f*). No. 40 moves across court ready to stop the offensive drive. As the driver shoots

34

Fig. 14, f-h:
Pick-Up
(defensive
weakside forward)

Fig. 14f

Fig. 14g   *Fig. 14h*

Fig. 14, i-k: **Pick-Up (defensive post)**

Fig. 14i   *Fig. 14j*   *Fig. 14k*

(*14g*), No. 40 goes up to block the shot. The original defender (No. 4), checks No. 40's man (*14h*) as the latter recovers his blocked shot.

This kind of play may also involve the defensive post man. *Figure 14i* (*see page 35*) shows offensive man (No. 4) driving on No. 11. As No. 4 gains an advantage (*14j*), the post defender moves in and holds his ground. Then, as No. 4 goes up for the lay-up shot, No. 31 makes the block and No. 11 checks the offensive post man off the backboard (*14k*).

This maneuver is the responsibility of the defensive man who is sloughing off his man. The player cannot fulfill this vital defensive obligation without (*1*) keeping the position of the ball within his vision and, (*2*) sloughing off his man so that he is in position to stop the offensive play.

Fig. 15, a-c: **Jump Switch**

Fig. 15a   Fig. 15b   Fig. 15c

Rule No. 7–The "jump switch," illustrated in Figure 15: This is a hard, aggressive switch by which we exert immediate pressure on the man with the ball. The switch must be made in the manner described. No. 11 starts across court on the dribble (*15a*) (*see above*). As he stands off to his teammate, No. 24 switches men (*15b*) and moves up hard on the man in possession as the other defender checks the cutter with his body (*15c*). As offensive player No. 3 alters his course, No. 24 will return to basic defensive position.

We make this play on all lateral back-court maneuvers by the offense which involve the ball. We find that most lateral offensive maneuvers are limited to the back-court. However, on lateral moves inside the circle, we prefer that our players stay with the man they are guarding, if at all possible. This play occurs most frequently on lateral slashes off a post. We want our defenders to squeeze between the two offensive players—the cutter and the post-man. We like to "hedge" on this type play and those

Fig. 16, a-f: "Hedging"

Fig. 16a

Fig. 16b

Fig. 16c

Fig. 16d   Fig. 16e   Fig. 16f

involving vertical offensive movements. "Hedging" occurs when the post defender moves out a step, or perhaps just fakes a step out and then moves back to play his own man. The effect of this maneuver is to slow up or halt the driver until his defender regains position. *Figure 16* (*see page 37*) illustrates a guard-forward post split. After the pass has been made to the post-man (*16 a,b*), No. 21 is successful in screening the side court defender (*16c*) so that he loses a step. The defensive post-man steps out to slow down the driver (*16d*), then recovers his man as each player checks his original man (*16 e,f*).

Figure 17 (*see below*) illustrates another possible play for the defensive man playing the driver off the post. Although we prefer the de-

Fig. 17, a-d:

Steal from Driver Off Side Post

Fig. 17a

Fig. 17b

Fig. 17c

Fig. 17d

fender playing the driver to squeeze between his man and the post, defensive man No. 13, realizing he is going to be rubbed off the post by his man's drive, slides behind the post on this play. (*Figure 17 a,b.*) The post defender loosens on his man to permit No. 13 to come through. No. 13 then comes through hard to steal (*17 c,d*) as the driver comes off the post. A sure-handed defensive man can make this play with very profitable results. If the driver stopped behind the screen on this play, No. 13 would hustle around the screen and recover position on his man. The post defender would then tighten on his man, ready to pick up the driver if he reverses the direction of his move.

We also encourage a hard, jump-switch on occasion by the defensive man who is playing the post. The same principle applies here as was mentioned in Rule No. 6. If the defender playing the side post jump-switches on a man coming off this post, it is the responsibility of the defender playing the driver to recover on the side post-man. This latter maneuver can be risky if there is a great differential in the height of the back-court and side-court defenders, since the bigger man can slide into deep post position with the smaller defender.

Rule No. 8–The double-up: In order to play a pressure game it is necessary to take a certain amount of risks in an effort to gain possession of the ball. One of the risks is the double-up, described in Chapter 2, "Individual Defense." As a team we want to be prepared for any double-up situation which occurs so that we won't get hurt by the move. Only practice will enable the individual player to learn what is a sound risk for him. This degree will vary considerably from individual to individual because the skills and natural aptitudes of the individuals vary con-

Fig. 18, a-c: **Man-to-Man Double-Up (team position)**

Fig. 18a

Fig. 18b

Fig. 18c

siderably. *Figures 6, 7,* and *8* have shown the techniques of doubling-up on the man with the ball. However, this tactic requires team cooperation and awareness. It remains for the three other defenders to cover up the defensive gap that has been created by sending two defenders after the one man with the ball. *Figure 18* illustrates the position required of these

Fig. 19, a-f: **Inside Pick-Up and Outside Recovery**

Fig. 19a

Fig. 19b

Fig. 19c

Fig. 19d   Fig. 19e   Fig. 19f

remaining defenders. *Figure 18a* shows defenders in their normal man-man pressure positions. As the two defensive guards effect the double-up (*18b*), the other defenders loosen to fill the gap temporarily created by the double-up (*18c*). If this tactic does not result in possession of the ball, the guard who left his man free to double-up on the ball must hustle back to pick up the open man. This brings us to the next principle to be observed in successful pressure play.

Rule No. 9–The inside recovery: This is a carry-over from the application of the "slough off and pick-up" rule. If the pressure game is to be successful it is imperative that each defensive man be alert to his responsibilities and willing to hustle to cover up and actually capitalize on efforts of the offensive team to take advantage of apparent gaps in the defense. Consistent application of these tactics often result in, what is to me, the greatest play in defensive basketball. It occurs when an aggressive defender has overplayed too much in his attempt to steal a pass (*19a*). His man moves to take advantage of his enthusiastic attempts and has gone for the basket (*19b*). The cutter is picked up inside (*19c*), and when he attempts to get the ball to the open offensive player on the baseline (*19d*), the ball is stolen by the initial defensive man (*19e*) who has recovered quickly (*19f*). The success of the pressure defense is dependent upon this kind of play.

Rule No. 10 is a summation of the first nine and injects a bit of philosophy which each player of the team must adopt. It emphasizes the fact that (*1*) the position of the ball is vitally important; (*2*) each player must strive to gain possession of the ball at every possible opportunity; (*3*) each player should feel free to take the calculated and sound risks necessary to gain possession.

Adherence to Rule No. 10 also requires the application of good, defensive rebounding principles. From the overplaying position, defenders

42

Fig. 20, a-e:
Roll and Block-Out

Fig. 20a

Fig. 20b

Fig. 20c

Fig. 20d

Fig. 20e

must make a definite move to roll back to the inside position and check their men off the board after an opponent's shot. *Figure 20* illustrates this aspect of defensive play. As the outside shot is taken (*20 a,b*), defensive men turn into their men and establish solid broad-based position (*20c*). In *20d* the ball has come off the left side of the basket, and the inside defensive men loosen somewhat in order to start for the ball. The last picture (*20e*) shows them making a definite move to get the rebound. This rebound positioning is essential if the overplaying team is to hold its own on the backboards.

The "calculated risk." It is easy to play a passive defensive game. It is easy to sit back and wait for the opponent to set up a pattern, and concede him position, the pass, and the shot. If this is the defensive philosophy you adopt, you can only hope that your opponent is missing his shots. It is my feeling that this is a lazy way of playing the game and that it must result in poor defense. The effective defense is a challenging defense—one that is willing to take a certain risk to obtain possession of the ball—one that is willing to challenge the opponent on every pass, on every dribble, and will limit greatly the number of good shots that the opponent takes in the game. The team with this attitude is the team that will win the big games and create the upsets. It will win because of its defense.

Flexibility of pressing man-to-man. The defense described in the earlier sections of this book is extremely flexible. Pressure defense may be played over a full-court, at three-quarter court, at half-court, or at the normal defensive position and it is still pressure defense. The determining factor of where the pressure is to be applied is the caliber of the opponent. If your opponent possesses ball-handlers who are too quick for full-court pressure, it is possible that pressure applied at half-court or at the top of the defensive circle will disrupt their offense entirely. This is still pressure defense and the same principles are applied. Regardless of where the pressure is applied, the defensive team wants to challenge every pass and to block off every passing lane. The pressing team must slough off men away from the ball, pick up free cutters, go after the interception of the pass, and hold position to draw the offensive charge. All of these factors are applicable regardless of where the pressing defense is played.

It has always been somewhat amusing to have individuals tell me after a game, "You won the game in the last 10 minutes with your press," or "Why did you wait until the last five minutes to begin your press?" Actually, it was often just a matter of positioning the press. Many individuals seem to feel that you are not playing a pressure defense unless you utilize the full-court press. This is hardly accurate. The objectives and the outcome which one may derive from pressure defense are attainable from any position on the court.

We have found, however, that if we can vary our man-to-man press with the zone press, the advantages increase immeasurably. Some opponents feel that if we play full-court man-to-man under the system described, we are, in effect, operating from a zone press. Of course, this is not true. While we will switch and, on occasion, double-up, the defense is still based upon man-to-man principles. The zone press operates from principles which are somewhat different.

COACHING TIPS

1. "Sell" players on the group benefits and responsibilities of pressure defense.

2. Emphasize the "watch-the-ball" defense.

3. Encourage the "go-for-the-ball" defense.

4. Emphasize sloughing off weak side players.

5. Praise the drawing of the offensive charge.

6. Encourage the attempt to steal, but *demand* the move to recover if the attempt fails.

7. Stress the overplay of the man but *demand* the vital roll-back to check opponents off the backboard.

8. Stress the immediate burst from defense to offense when possession of the ball is obtained.

CHAPTER 4

The Zone Press

Any defensive structure requires some variety for success. The pressing defense is no exception. Applying man-to-man pressure at different points on the court is helpful; sometimes that much variation is sufficient to keep the opponent's offense in check. At other times such change may be inadequate and another defensive variation is necessary. On these occasions, I have found the zone press to be of great value.

Zone press principles. There are many types of zone press. All of them, however, operate on certain principles. These principles will hold true regardless of the type of press used:

1. Play the ball.
2. Double-up on the man with the ball at every opportunity.
3. Force the opponent into a "bad-pass" position.
4. Tie up the man with the ball or force a five-second, held ball situation.
5. Intercept or deflect any pass the defender feels he can get a hand on.
6. Steal the ball from the man in possession.
7. Players not involved with a double-up must slough off and protect the most vulnerable areas against offensive attack.
8. Hustle to exert constant pressure on opponent, but *don't foul.*

Whatever type of press a coach intends to use, he must first explain these basic principles to his players. He must be certain the players understand them. Then he is better able to explain the shifts and player responsibilities of his particular choice of zone press.

Importance of the double-up. The technique of the double-up has been described earlier. Since it is the most vital aspect of the zone press, however, it is necessary to elaborate on this tactic. A good zone press will have a constant double-up in progress. The players involved in this action must approach the man with the ball aggressively, but, at the same time, they must be careful not to commit a personal foul. These players should obtain position as close to the man in possession as possible, wedging him into the "V" described earlier, without making contact with him. They must make use of their arms and legs to harass their opponent and to get a "piece of the ball," since any slight deflection may result in possession of the ball for the defensive team. They should shout, lunge at the man, contort their faces—using every tactic at their disposal to disconcert the player with the ball.

Players involved in the double-up must exercise care so that the man with the ball does not split them with his dribble. If the defenders approach the player in possession so that he is forced into the pocket, they are then in a good position to stop his dribble. The gap between them should be so narrow that the dribbler would be reluctant to attempt such a risky maneuver.

If the man with the ball has not dribbled, the defenders should close the apex of the "V" to an even greater degree. If the double-up men bring their inside feet to a position almost touching each other and drop their corresponding hands, they will be able to prevent the break-through by the dribbler.

There is a great psychological factor at work in the zone press. The more the defensive team utilizes this factor, the greater the success of the press. Players actually involved in the double-up may perform successfully even though they never touch the ball if they can force the opponent into a hurried, inaccurate pass.

The players not involved in the double-up look to deflect or intercept the pass. They also have a responsibility to protect the vulnerable areas of the court so the opponent will not come up with the easy field goal.

THE 3-1-1 ZONE PRESS

The zone press I have found to be most serviceable is also the least used in college competition. It is the 3-1-1. We have used this type of zone press each year of my coaching experience at St. Joseph's. It has worked so successfully that there has been no reason to change to another formation. The 3-1-1 is easy to teach. The shifts are basically sound and logically consistent. Our players have confidence in it because it has stood up to the test of tough competition and passed with flying colors.

Positions. In any zone press alignment, it is necessary for the coach and player to use common terminology so that communication between them is facilitated. The first thing to consider is the player positions. I have found it helpful to number the positions and assign names to the men playing these positions.

Diagram 2 shows the positions of the 3-1-1 set over full-court. The No. 1 position is played by the "middle" man. The "wing" men play the No. 2 and 3 positions. The No. 4 position is played by the "first deep" man; the "second deep" player fills the No. 5 position.

Using this terminology to designate positions, we are able to communicate easily with the players by referring to position numbers or the name of the man playing a particular position. We use these terms in shouting instructions to players during the course of the game. This often obviates the necessity of calling time-out to make an adjustment in the defense.

Player responsibilities. Once the player positions are understood, the next assignment concerns the responsibilities of each position. Although players will know their particular positions best, they should be familiar with the responsibilities of the other players for complete understanding of the press.

Diagram No. 2

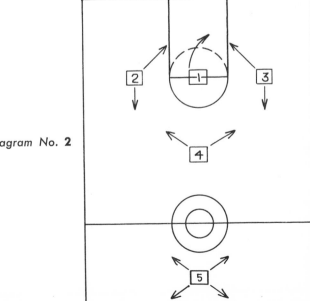

Middle or No. 1 position

1. Guide the direction of a pass or the dribbler to a position favorable to the defense.
2. Double-up on the man in possession when the ball is on the front line to his right or left.
3. Protect the middle area of the press when the ball is on the sides or in the deep position.
4. Anticipate and deflect or intercept passes at any position on the court as the "drifter."

The wing or No. 2 and No. 3 positions

1. Guide the direction of the dribbler into the front pocket.
2. Prevent the short loop pass over the front line position.
3. Double-up on the man with the ball when he is (a) on his side of front line, (b) on his side of the court at the side or corner position.
4. Protect under the basket area when the ball is over mid-court and is in the opposite corner.
5. Protect the lower foul lane area when the ball is over mid-court and is at the opposite side-court position.
6. Rebound aggressively.

First deep or No. 4 position

1. Prevent pass to high post position to the rear of front line.
2. Double-up on man with the ball at side-court position.
3. Protect deep lane position when ball is over mid-court and in corners.
4. Rebound aggressively.

Second deep or No. 5 position

1. Protect under the basket area against long or short lay-up pass.
2. Prevent pass to long post position (especially in full-court press).
3. Move out to cover and double-up on man with ball in either corner.
4. Rebound aggressively.

Full-court zone press. While the shifts and objectives of the zone press are similar regardless of the position on the court at which it is applied, there are some factors regarding the full-court application which require amplification.

Although the effort must be greater (and the risks increase proportionately), the benefits of this tactic may accrue by the basketfull. I have seen great leads melt away to nothing in a matter of minutes through the use of the full-court zone press. When successful, it generates an enthusiastic force which is often invincible.

The shifts of the 3-1-1 full-court press. *Diagram 2* illustrates the initial alignment of the 3-1-1 full-court press. We start our front line across the foul line until the first pass is made. We do this to encourage the first pass to be made inside the front line. The player with the ball out of bounds will usually accommodate us rather than risk a pass into more closely defended regions.

No. 4 takes the initial position just inside mid-court and looks for the nearest offensive player behind the front line. No. 5 takes position between mid-court and the top of the defensive foul circle, then looks for the "long" offensive man.

The front line will also try to influence the direction of the first pass if it seems advantageous to do so. In most instances we will try to direct the ball to the offensive team's left since, generally speaking, players do not operate as efficiently in that direction. If we play a team whose backcourt leader is lefthanded, we will direct the ball to the right. We strive to place the first receiver in an immediately "weak" position from which to operate, so that his dribble and his pass are affected.

Once the pass-in is made, there is an immediate double team on the ball (*Diagram 3*). No. 1 and No. 3 rush the man in possession, intent on

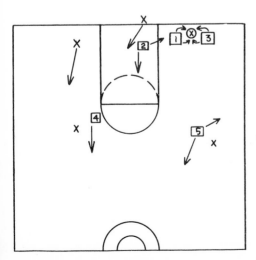

Diagram No. 3

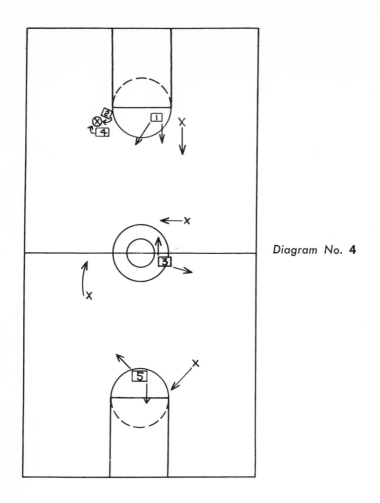

Diagram No. 4

preventing his advancement with the ball and trying to force him to throw a lob pass. No. 2 has become the "drifter," looking to halt a give-and-go from the first passer, or to pick off any soft pass. No. 5 comes out hard and overplays the deep man on his side of the court. No. 4 plays between the other offensive players and is the safety man against any long pass.

Diagram 4 shows the offensive team getting the ball to the backcourt post position. No. 4 and No. 2 double-up on the ball, No. 5 quickly retreats and becomes the safety man, and No. 1 and No. 3 look for lob passes either to deflect of intercept.

With the ball over half-court (*Diagram 5*), No. 2 and No. 1 double-up, No. 3 becomes the drifter, No. 4 overplays the high post-man, and No. 5 is ready to move in either direction to cover the baseline.

Once the ball is over mid-court, the rules for the half-court zone press are in effect. We continue to operate under the same general principles, however, doubling-up on each pass receiver and attempting to force the opponent into a ball-handling error which will give us possession.

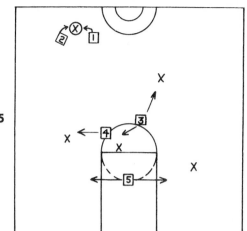

Diagram No. 5

Half-court 3-1-1 zone press. When we start to zone press full-court, we stay in it after the opponent crosses the mid-court line. Occasionally, when the opponent advances the ball over mid-court, we get caught in situations in which our player positioning is not ideal. Often the No. 5 player is drawn out of position to cover a high post. The wingman opposite the ball then must cover for him temporarily under the basket. Players then return to the basic positions shown in *Diagram 6* as quickly as possible.

This is the formation used when starting the press at mid-court. The No. 1 man takes position at the mid-court line flanked by No. 2 and No. 3 who are a few steps closer to the baseline than the No. 1 man. This position is taken to lure the dribbler *over* mid-court and into the "pocket" between No. 1 and the wingmen. No. 4 takes initial position at the top of the foul circle and No. 5 at the dotted line of the foul circle.

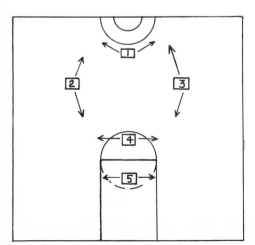

Diagram No. 6

No. 1 forces the ball to whichever side of the court he chooses, again keeping in mind the dribbling proficiency of the ball-handlers.

The other players utilize faking techniques in order to discourage the first pass over the front line. No. 3 darts back and forth as indicated in the diagram. No. 4 stations himself initially so that a pass to the high post is discouraged. Once No. 1 and No. 2 have cornered the man with the ball in the pocket which they have created, they try to force him into a hurried, inaccurate pass. The other defenders, especially No. 4 and No. 3, are alert to intercept that pass. (*See Diagram 7.*)

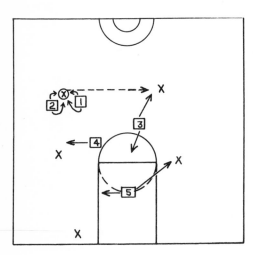 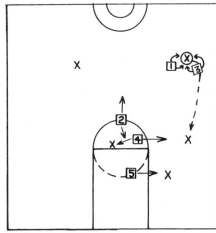

Diagram No. 7   Diagram No. 8

Assuming the passer was able to get the ball safely to his fellow back-court man, No. 1 chases over to join No. 3 in doubling-up on player now in possession, No. 2 becomes the "drifter" and No. 4 moves back to cover the high post once more. (*See Diagram 8.*)

If the ball is passed to the side-court, as in *Diagram 9*, No. 4 moves out to double-up with No. 3. No. 1 becomes the drifter. No. 2 fills the high post spot, while No. 5 still protects that most vulnerable area under the basket.

If the ball goes to the corner, No. 5 comes out and covers that player along with No. 3 (*Diagram 10*). No. 2 has dropped all the way under the basket, No. 4 retreats to the foul lane area to cut off that passing lane while No. 1 looks for the lob pass to the back-court.

The next sequence (*Diagram 11*) shows the ball inside the zone on the baseline. This situation is dangerous and should be avoided if possible.

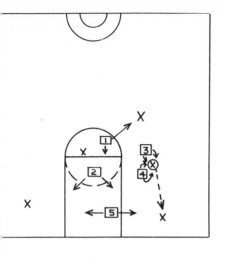 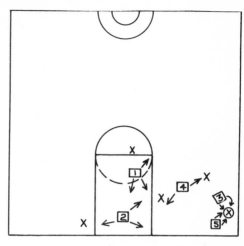

Diagram No. 9   Diagram No. 10

No. 4 should play this man from the front and cut off the pass from the corner, while No. 2 covers under the basket. Sometimes the post man will get position, however. If he does and No. 5 is in the corner, No. 5 and No. 4 double-up, No. 2 protects underneath while No. 1 and No. 3 look to pick off the possible pass-out attempt.

(*Note:* The entire sequence of these shifts in the half-court zone press is illustrated in *Figure 21—see page 56.* The same defensive moves described by *Diagrams 6-11* are pictorially represented in this figure.)

Diagram No. 11

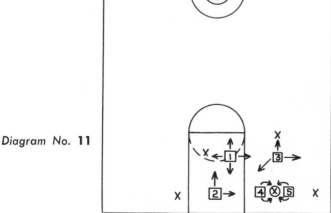

Fig. 21, a-k: **Zone Press (half-court)**

Fig. 21a

Fig. 21b

Fig. 21c

Fig. 21d

Fig. 21e

Fig. 21f

Fig. 21g

Fig. 21h

Fig. 21i

Fig. 21j

Fig. 21k

The element of "risk." Those are the basic shifts in the 3-1-1 zone press as we practice them at St. Joseph's. Our over-all objective is to gain possession of the ball. We attempt to do this by applying the greatest amount of pressure possible on the ball with the least amount of risk. In order to accomplish this, we feel we must be protected under the basket at all times. The foul lane, the second most vulnerable area, also must be covered. We realize we must give up some shots if we are going to double-up on the ball each time it is passed. The areas most accessible are the sides and corners (*Diagram 12*). Since this is also the least desirable shot to take, we feel we are operating under the best conditions possible.

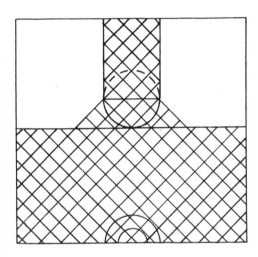

Diagram No. **12**

Remember that the shifts in the 3-1-1 are basically the same whether played at half-court, three-quarter court, or full-court. Circumstances of the particular game, caliber of the opponent, pressing ability of team personnel, and other factors determine the extent of the press.

The 3-1-1 pressing zone is not a panacea. There are times when our opponents have beaten it, but in such instances we have felt that we would have lost the game anyway. We have called upon the 3-1-1 in close to 50 percent of our games and it has enabled us to win a great many games which were apparently "down the drain." Like all pressing zones, it is a defense which tolerates no loafing. There must be a 100 percent effort from all players. If one player doesn't do his job to the fullest, the smart offensive team will score easy field goals.

The fact that we have used only the 3-1-1 zone press at St. Joseph's does not mean that I feel other zone presses are without merit. We have been pressed by other zone formations and some have given us a great deal of trouble. The two zone presses (other than the 3-1-1) which seem to have the most strength are the 2-2-1 and the 1-2-2. Each has been successfully tested in college competition. Both are basically sound pressing alignments. So that coaches may decide for themselves which offers the greatest benefits for their particular situation, the shifts and player responsibilities of these two defenses are presented here.

THE 2-2-1 ZONE PRESS

Strengths and weaknesses. The 2-2-1 press affords the defensive team good coverage along the front line, the side-court area, and under the basket. It offers good double-up opportunities at the front and side positions. If a team has a good, active big man (or a player who can play the big man's role) to play the deep position, this press can be extremely effective. With such a player underneath, the front and wing positions can take many more defensive chances, knowing there is strong support to the rear. The 2-2-1 may be used to advantage over full, three-quarter, or half-court.

While this zone is strong at the side positions (a weakness of the 3-1-1), it is weak in the middle area. Wingmen must be very active, with keen anticipation to compensate for this shortcoming. They must work well with the deep man to cover the high post and still maintain protection underneath the basket. Lacking the big man described above, the value of this zone is limited.

Player responsibilities in 2-2-1 zone press. The responsibilities of each player in the 2-2-1 press are as follows:

The front or No. 1 and No. 2 positions

1. Overplay the potential pass receivers in their respective areas on the throw-in pass from out of bounds.
2. Halt the advance of the ball and double-up together on the player in possession at the front line position.
3. Double-up with the wingman on the player in possession when the ball is on their side of the court.
4. Protect the middle area of the press when the opposite front man and wingman are doubling up on the ball.
5. Anticipate and deflect or intercept passes at any position on the court as a "drifter."

The wing or No. 3 and No. 4 positions

1. Overplay potential pass receivers in their areas on the throw-in from out of bounds.
2. Halt the advance of the ball and double-up with the corresponding front man on the player in possession when the ball is at the side-court.
3. Double-up with the deep man when the player in possession is behind the wing position on the same side of the court.
4. Protect the deep court area when the ball is on the opposite side-court position.
5. Assume the "safety" position (under the basket) when the deep man and the opposite wingman are in a double-up.

The deep or No. 5 position

1. Play the safety position—protecting the basket area against the easy field goal.
2. Guard against the long pass from out of bounds.
3. Double-up with the appropriate wingman when the ball is in the deep position (behind the wingman).
4. Rebound aggressively.

Shifts of the 2-2-1. *Diagram 13a* shows the basic set-up of the 2-2-1. Contrasted to the 3-1-1, defensive men No. 1 and No. 2 overplay the opponents in their respective areas to prevent their receiving the throw-in from out of bounds. The No. 3 and No. 4 men cut off the passing lanes

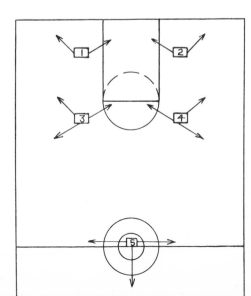

Diagram No. 13a

to players in their areas (including the high post at the back-court foul line). The No. 5 man plays the safety position to discourage the long pass to a down-court cutter. The No. 5 man also backs up the No. 3 or No. 4 man if this becomes necessary to stop the opponent's advancement.

Diagram 13b illustrates the shifts required following the short pass-in and vertical up-court dribble by the opponent. No. 1 and No. 3 form the double-up. No. 2 becomes the "drifter," looking for the same steal opportunities as in the 3-1-1. No. 4 overplays the high post, and while No. 5 moves over to replace No. 3, he is still responsible for the protection of the back-court.

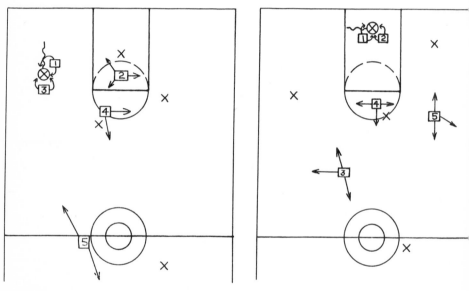

Diagram No. 13b   Diagram No. 13c

Diagram 13c illustrates the short pass-in and a subsequent lateral dribble toward the No. 2 man, No. 2 joins No. 1 in the double-up and the other players shift to the right side of the court. No. 4, playing the high post, stays with that assignment, but moves to his right to stay between his man and the ball. No. 5 moves to cut off the outlet to his right and No. 3 becomes the safety man.

Diagrams 14 through 18 (see pages 63 and 64) show the shifts demanded by the 2-2-1 in a pass-to-pass sequence originating with Diagram 13b.

Diagram 14 shows the pass received by the post man in No. 5's area. No. 5 stops the advance of the ball and is joined by No. 3 in the double-up.

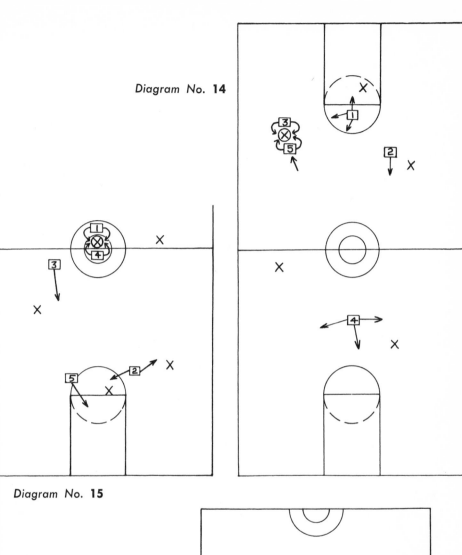

Diagram No. 14

Diagram No. 15

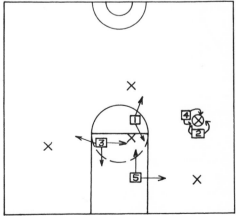

Diagram No. 16

No. 1 becomes the drifter; No. 4 covers the middle area, still protecting the back-court; and No. 2 hustles back to cover the exposed right side-court.

Diagram 15 shows the pass made to the high post in front of No. 4, who checks the advance of the ball at that point. He is joined by No. 1 in the double-up; No. 3 becomes the drifter; and No. 2 checks the deep position as No. 5 hustles back to provide added protection.

With the next pass to the side-court (*Diagram 16*), No. 4 and No. 2 double-up, No. 1 becomes the drifter, No. 3 covers the upper lane area, and No. 5 has returned to his "goal-tender" role. If the opponent is successful in getting the ball to the high post in the lane area (*Diagram 17*) No. 1 and No. 3 double-up, No. 4 drops back to his deep position, No. 2 is the drifter, and No. 5 moves to the left side of the lane.

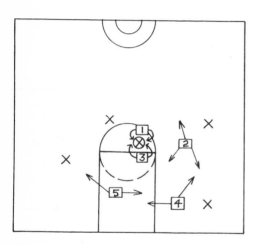

Diagram No. 17

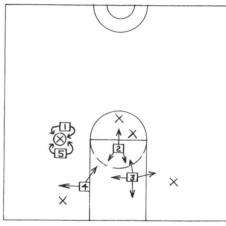

Diagram No. 18

If the high post succeeds in getting the ball to a weak side teammate (*Diagram 18*), No. 5 must come up to stop the play. No. 1 will come over to double-up, No. 4 replaces No. 5 under the hoop, and No. 3 drops back to the "deep away" position. This is one of the few times it is necessary to take No. 5 from the deep position, but on such an offensive move, there is no choice. When players are drawn out of position like this, they should return to original responsibilities as soon as it is safely possible.

THE 1-2-2 ZONE PRESS

Strengths and weaknesses. The 1-2-2 press is strong around the perimeter. The front line and the side areas are well protected and afford ample double-up opportunities. When used over full-court, it is possible to apply pressure to the man with the ball out of bounds. Teams with an especially quick-handed player of more than average height may find the No. 1 position (*see Diagram 20 on page 67*) an excellent spot for this performer, tight on the opponent out of bounds. I have seen such a player in this position rattle his opponent to such an extent that he has thrown the ball right into the defender's hands for easy scoring opportunities. Teams pressing from the 1-2-2 formation are well positioned to fast-break as soon as they obtain possession. Another possible advantage of this press is that the shifts are very similar to those of the straight 1-2-2 zone defense. The teaching process is thereby facilitated for those teams which use the 1-2-2 as any part of their defense.

The outstanding weakness of this press is in the middle area. As true with the 2-2-1, there must be a high degree of team play between the wingmen and the deep men for this weakness to be concealed. It is difficult to restrict the play of the good post-man with this type of press. Such a player can be used to relay passes to the cutters going to the basket.

Player responsibilities in 1-2-2 zone press. The responsibilities of each player in the 1-2-2 press are as follows:

The middle or No. 1 position

1. Play tight on the man with the ball out of bounds in the backcourt, leaping up, waving the arms, anticipating his moves in an effort to deflect or intercept the pass-in.
2. Double-up on the man in possession whenever the ball is on the front line; this double-up often is made from behind the offensive player.
3. Protect the middle area of the press when the wing and deep men are doubling-up on the ball.
4. Anticipate and deflect or intercept passes at any position on the court as a "drifter."

The wing or No. 2 and No. 3 positions

1. Halt the advance of the man with the ball on the appropriate sides of the court.

2. Double-up with the middle man when the ball is on the same side of the court and in front of the wing position.
3. Double-up with the corresponding deep man when the ball is on the same side of the court and behind the wing position.
4. Play the "drifter" when the opposite wingman is doubling-up with the middle man.
5. Protect under the basket when the opposite wingman and opposite deep man are doubling-up on the ball.

The deep or No. 4 and No. 5 positions

1. Guard against the easy field goal in the under the basket area.
2. Cover the middle of the press against the post play when the ball is in front of the opposite wing position.
3. Double-up with the corresponding wingman when the ball is behind the wing position on the same side of the court.
4. Cut off the passing lane to the deep post when the opposite deep man and opposite wingman are doubling-up.
5. Intercept or deflect loop pass to offensive players being face-guarded by No. 2 and No. 3 players.
6. Rebound aggressively.

Shifts of the 1-2-2. The 1-2-2 full-court press formation is shown in *Diagram 19a*. The No. 1 man plays the ball out of bounds, No. 2 and No. 3 men overplay and face-guard the opponent in their respective areas, and No. 4 and No. 5 men cut off the passing lanes to any deep offensive player.

If the opponent puts two men up front to receive the pass-in, and one on the post position in the middle area of the press (*Diagram 19b*),

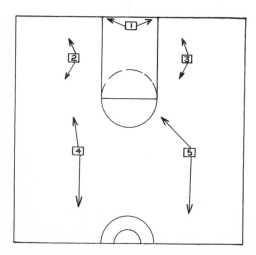

Diagram No. **19a**

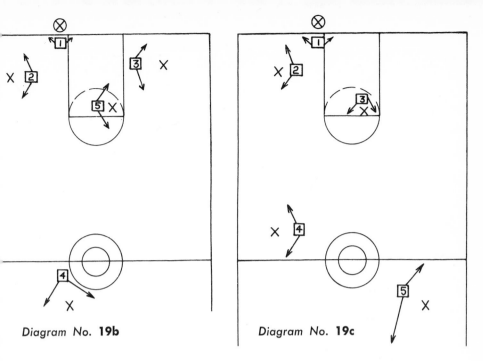

Diagram No. **19b**

Diagram No. **19c**

No. 2 and No. 3 overplay the front men. The "deep away" man, No. 5, covers the high post. No. 4 plays the deep safety position.

If the opponent puts only one man up front to receive the pass-in, *Diagram 19c,* the wingman on the same side as the opponent overplays, and the opposite wingman (No. 3 in this instance) checks the post position. This leaves the No. 4 and No. 5 men to cover the long pass.

Diagram 20 shows the ball in front of the No. 2 man. No. 1 comes back to double-up with No. 2; No. 3 becomes the drifter; No. 4 moves up to help on the same side of the court, and No. 5 protects the long pass.

Diagram No. **20**

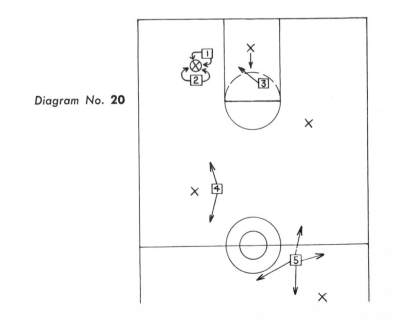

The next pass is made up-court in front of the No. 4 man. No. 2 joins No. 4 in the double-up; No. 1 drops off to become the drifter; and No. 3 and No. 5 cover the rear flank positions. (*Diagram 21*)

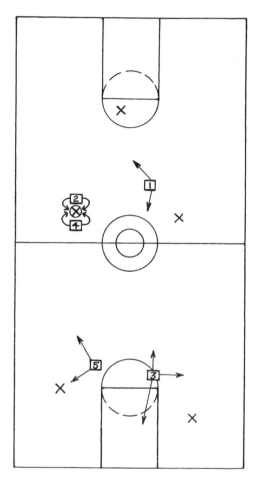

Diagram No. **21**

In *Diagram 22,* the ball has advanced over mid-court. No. 1 and No. 3 double-up on the ball; No. 4 covers the high post position; No. 2 drops back to cover underneath the basket, if necessary, and No. 5 overplays the corner on the side of the ball.

With the ball in the high post position (*Diagram 23, see page 69*), No. 1 and No. 4 double-up; No. 2 drops all the way underneath the basket; No. 3 overplays the outlet pass on his side of the court; and No. 5 protects the deep position on his side of the court.

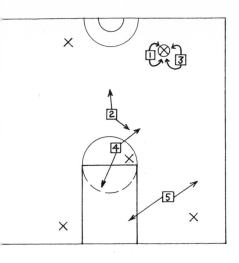

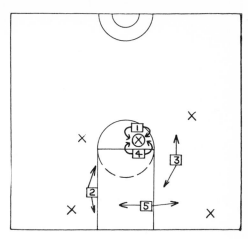

Diagram No. **22**

Diagram No. **23**

Finally, with the ball in the corner (*Diagram 24*), No. 3 and No. 5 double-up; No. 4 cuts off the passing lane to the deep post position; No. 2 protects the basket area; and No. 1 is the drifter, looking for any pass he can get a hand on.

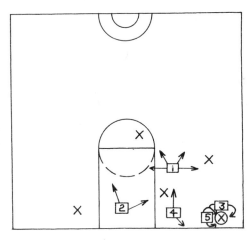

Diagram No. **24**

COACHING TIPS

1. Stress careful compliance with press shifts at all times.
2. Drill players in all zone press positions they may be required to play in the game.

3. Practice "double-up" situations from all areas of the court to improve their effectiveness.
4. Encourage players to take "good risks" to deflect or intercept pass.
5. Stress exaggerated movements and shouting by pressers to fluster opponents.

CHAPTER 5

Adjustment of Available Material to the Pressing Defense

Coaches should formulate their defensive plans for a season in the same manner with which offensive plans are made. Height, speed, agility, stamina, tenacity, and other such personal factors must go into the determination of the basic defense. Some coaches don't seem to concern themselves beyond the preparation of a basic defense. Such a practice is bound to cost them ball games. Even if the coach is not convinced of the value of the pressure defense as his fundamental alignment, he must consider the press at least for emergency measures. There are many occasions during the course of a season that demand the pressing type defense. These situations will be considered in the next chapter, "Strategic Use of the Pressing Defense."

Coaches often feel that they just don't get the kind of material required to effectively operate the pressing defense. I can't agree. I am convinced that there is some kind of press suitable for any type of material which the coach has on hand. Let's consider the material needed for the press and some of the adjustments necessitated by the lack of ideal personnel.

FULL-COURT MAN-TO-MAN PRESS

The guards. The primary requisite for this type of pressing defense is to have at least two well-conditioned, quick-moving, tenacious guards. These must be boys who love to play defense and are dedicated to the task of stopping the dribbler, overplaying their men, and stealing the ball. Two or three such players among a team's personnel can lead an effective full-court press with only a moderate amount of skilled helpers. This is a tough job, but one which has great appeal to the real scrappers or "pepperpots" of the team. If this type of back-court personnel is not available, I would hesitate to include a full-court man-to-man press in the pre-season defensive plans. For if the defensive back-court cannot contain the offensive guards, the guards will get through and the way is open for the easy field goal.

As far as size is concerned, it seems that the small player does a better job than the tall boy in this capacity. For the past two years we have been using a crew of four guards in this role ranging in size from 5'8" to 6'0". We have been well-pleased with the results. These small men are especially effective in checking the progress of the dribbler in the back-court—an extremely vital aspect of the press. Their short stature, which enables them to stay low on the dribbler, proves to be an asset in this regard.

This defense gives the coach an opportunity to utilize the usually abundant supply of little men who ordinarily might be overlooked because of their size. If given the opportunity, these players often return great dividends to the investor.

The forwards. The defensive forwards must have many of the same characteristics as the guards if the full-court man-to-man press is to be effective. The forwards must be fast, aggressive, and possess relatively quick movements. Size is not of great consequence. We have found that since we are taking the offensive forwards away from the backboard by our pressing tactics, we can hold our own rebounding even though we are giving up several inches in height. We have been able to use 6'2" and 6'3" defensive forwards against 6'6" men and we feel that it has worked to our advantage. Of course, if bigger men were available who could do the job of defensing, they would be preferred. Usually, however, the bigger men are less agile and a bit slower in their movements and, consequently, are not as proficent in the press. So, as with the guards, the important factor is playing the position well. Forwards must overplay the outlet to the side-court, make effective switches, and be alert to capture errant passes.

The center. This is the second most vital position in the full-court man-to-man press. This player must be aggressive and a good leaper and rebounder. He must possess a keen sense of anticipation, and, if possible, develop the knack of blocking the short shot after it leaves the hand of the shooter. Again, height is not the all-important factor, but the bigger the man with these talents, the better he should be. During a recent season, we played a great many games with a 6'3" center. This player had extraordinary leaping ability, and a fine sense of timing for blocking the short shot. By pressing our opponent full- or three-quarter court, we were able to bring the offensive big man (often 6'8" to 6'10") away from the basket where our 6'3" man could play him effectively.

HALF-COURT MAN-TO-MAN PRESS

If the players on a particular squad do not meet the requirements cited above for the full-court press, they may be equally tough pressing half-court. This press can be effective although the players are a step slow and not quite as quick as the coach might prefer.

The guards. If the guards are not lightning quick, they may still get a great deal of profit from a half-court press. In this technique, the guards must make up for their lack of speed by the finesse of body checking, the deftness of their switches, their ability to flick the ball away from the dribbler, and their over-all alertness. Since the defensive guard does not have to go full-court, he has more help from his teammates in slowing down and stopping the dribbler, and in picking up the loose offensive man who may have overpowered the guard with speed. The ball-handler must still be stopped, but it is considerably easier to do this at mid-court than at some point in the back-court.

The forwards. If the defensive forwards are not quick enough to press full-court, they must be more the equal of their opponents in size to press half-court. Since the offensive forwards will obtain position closer to the backboard, the corresponding defensive player must be able to rebound with him better than is demanded by the full-court press.

Like the guards, the forwards' responsibilities are much the same with the full-court press. The difference lies in the more limited area of operation and the consequent help the defender derives from his nearer teammates. Generally speaking, the forwards may be slower but should be stronger off the boards at half-court pressing than with full-court. The personal attributes of aggressiveness, determination, and dedication to the task remain the same for both types of press.

The center. The closer the defense is to the basket, the greater the demands placed upon the defensive center. While it is possible for the physically mismatched center to hold his own if his team presses effectively in the back-court, this type player is easily dominated at a conservative defensive position. Therefore, the center of the team pressing at half-court must be bigger and stronger than his counterpart who presses full-court. As with the other positions, he may be a bit slower. The more defensive skills he possesses (overplaying, shot blocking, picking-up), the more valuable he will be to his team.

Summary. In general, then, it may be said that the greater the team speed the larger the area of the court over which the pressing man-to-man defense may be exerted. The guards hold the key to the successful man-to-man press. With great speed and agility at this position, the full-court press will be effective. With something short of these qualities, the half-court man-to-man press or the zone press can be brought into play—often with equal effectiveness.

The coach is often faced with the necessity of utilizing personnel lacking the ideal qualifications for man-to-man pressing when the game situation demands that defense. He may want to get a small, good shooter into the lineup although he is slow afoot and an ineffective back-court presser. Perhaps this player can be used to press a bigger opponent who is more his equal in speed. Since the offensive team is pulled away from the backboard by the effective press, this move may be made without a great deal of risk to the pressing team, and, at the same time, it increases the team's scoring power.

The same type of move may be made by the coach in sending his defensive forward against the opponent's big center. The coach's tactics will be determined by the personnel of the opponent and the offensive demands of his team at the time. He must be ready to make the necessary adjustments with his personnel and the players must be prepared for these moves. The only way for them to be prepared is by practicing game situations in which these moves are experienced.

THE ZONE PRESS

The zone press requires a smaller degree of specialization than the man-to-man press. By this I mean that it is possible to operate an effective zone press with less defensive ability than is required for the man-to-man press. The zone press affords the coach the opportunity to "hide" some slow moving personnel (not too many, however) and still get an effective job done.

Ideally, of course, the zone press will operate most effectively with topnotch personnel. The general qualities sought for each of the positions are described here:

The middle man or No. 1 position. This player is the "quarterback" of the zone press. It is his responsibility to guide the general direction of offensive play so that it is favorable for the defensive team. He must have quick hands and be fleet afoot. He should be a deft ball thief and possess a fine sense of anticipation. He need not be a tall player since he rarely is drawn into position under the defensive basket. This is an ideal spot for the little dynamo who is so often a great team leader. Since this player is out front on defense most of the time, this is a good spot for the player adept at leading the fast break.

Although the player with characteristics described above functions best at the No. 1 position, we have used a slow player in this spot on occasion in order to get a good shooter into the lineup. Since this player's movements are limited to a lateral direction and he has help on either side from the wingmen, a slow man can be utilized here in an emergency without damaging the effectiveness of the press too much.

The wingmen or the No. 2 and No. 3 positions. Wingmen should have good speed, quick hands and reflexes, and be big enough to do an adequate job of rebounding on the defensive board. Great size is not an essential characteristic, however. It is possible in good college competition to get away with players ranging in size from 6'0" to 6'3" who are good leapers and who like to battle under the backboards. The deficit in size is often more than compensated for by the increase in speed and agility. If one is forced to use a small player in one of the wing positions, it is a better risk to use him in the No. 2 position than No. 3, inasmuch as most teams shoot more from the *right side* of the court than the left. This factor permits the small men to be outside when the shot is taken rather than under the basket.

In an important part of a crucial game which I recall, St. Joseph's used 5'8" men in both the No. 1 and No. 2 positions, and 6'0" men in both the No. 3 and No. 4 positions while operating the 3-1-1 press. This group, pressing three-quarter court, was so pesky that the opponent's big men were forced to come out near mid-court to advance the ball. As the big men came farther away from the back-board, their size became less of an asset and their ball-handling deficiencies became magnified. We were able to overcome an apparently insurmountable second-half deficit and win the game going away. That this seemingly ridiculous patchwork line-up worked successfully was a tribute to the aggressiveness and the tremendously quick reactions of these players.

The deep men or the No. 4 and No. 5 positions. The deep men are usually the two biggest in the lineup. Generally, the more agile of the two plays the No. 4 position; the stronger and slower man plays the No. 5 spot. Both must be good rebounders. The No. 4 man should possess a good sense of anticipation. This is especially needed in guarding the post positions at the circle or at the side-court. As has been stated, it is possible to use a smaller man in this position in an emergency. He may be able to steal enough from the post men to make his presence worthwhile.

The No. 5 man is the best rebounder. It helps tremendously if this man has acquired the knack of blocking that short shot lay-up or jumper. He is the protector of the basket—the goal tender, if you will. His presence is vital. There is nothing more demoralizing to the press than to have an enemy score an unmolested lay-up after the defense has been chasing itself to the point of exhaustion in quest of the ball. The defense takes on added confidence with a big, tough No. 5 man.

Coaches must work diligently with the players who come closest to fulfilling the qualities demanded by this position. Almost every squad will have a player who can leap a bit better and time the ball to a greater degree than his teammates. Weight training and the isometric regimens will help to develop these traits. The coach must use the best he has for this purpose —regardless of the height of the player. The average player, who otherwise might be of little value to his team, can be a lifesaver if he can develop into an adequate No. 5 man.

Summary. As stated, in relation to the man-to-man press, the better the pressing material, the farther into the back-court one may extend the press. If material is limited (and it always seems to be), then the extent of the zone press will have to be shortened.

Even with ideal material, there are certain benefits to be derived from shifting the press from full- to half-court from time to time during the course of the game. It keeps the offensive team guessing and requires them to change their mode of attack. Such change often brings favorable results to the defensive team.

COACHING TIPS

1. Analyze the pressing ability of team personnel as early in the season as possible.

2. Single out key personnel for the key positions in the press and work diligently with them.
3. Use the practice session to determine the type press best suited to your personnel.
4. Use fundamental drills to improve the ball-hawking skills of players.

CHAPTER 6

Strategic Use
of the
Pressing Defense

Control tempo of game. Aside from the stated objectives
of forcing the opponent from his planned style of play
and obtaining quick possession of the ball, the pressing
defenses afford other benefits to the team which uses
them wisely. The pressing defense can be used to *control the tempo of the
game.* If, for example, the opponent wants to play a deliberate game but
the defense counteracts this objective with a pressing, demanding, hurry-
up style, it is extremely difficult for the offensive team to carry out its
planned attack. If, on the other hand, the opponent is a fast-breaking team
and plays a running type game, the pressing defense may actually be used
to *slow down the pace.* This may seem contradictory, but if one analyzes
the component parts of the break and the factors on which it relies for
success, use of the pressing defense to stop fast breaks will not seem too
ludicrous.

The principal objective of most fast-breaking teams is to get the ball
off the defensive backboard and then out quickly to the front line. However, if pressure is applied to the rebounder, and the players attempting to
receive the outlet pass are overplayed, it will be difficult for the offensive
team to start its fast-break from that vantage point.

If the fast-breaking team relies on the long pass or a quick pitch-out after a field goal or foul shot and the outlets are closed off, it will be impossible for the team to initiate its break in this manner. If a team is a helter-skelter, long-passing team and the pass receivers are overplayed, then it will be difficult for them to start the break in that manner. A team may also apply pressure at the normal defensive position—allowing the opponent to bring the ball up rapidly and then exert pressure to slow down the fast-breaking team.

In any event, the *tempo* of the game is controlled by the *defensive team* and the best manner for control is through the exertion of pressure at some point on the court. It is left to the coach of the particular team, in evaluating his opponents, to determine how he may best control the tempo of the game.

Surprise element. Another strategic use of the pressing defense is through the *unexpected use of the press.* On occasion we have started the game with an all-out, aggressive, risk-taking, full-court zone press and have found it to have an electrifying effect on our opponent.

On other occasions we have reserved the use of the zone press and brought it into play for as little as 10 seconds in a game and it often gave us the desired possession of the ball.

We have had some success by alternating our man-to-man and zone presses so the offense wasn't quite sure which type of press we were using. When we found that our opponent was having some success in solving the defense of one kind, we have switched to another and rotated back and forth through the use of hand signals from the bench.

A simple set of finger signals, given by the coach to his floor leader when play has stopped temporarily (free throw, jump ball, substitution) or even after possession of the ball is obtained by his team in the back-court, will suffice. We designate defenses by number. Number 3 refers to the 3-1-1 zone press, number 2 to the 1-2-2 standard zone, number 1 to the 1-3-1 zone press, and number 5 to the man-to-man. The coach gives the signal and points to the area of the court where he wants the defense to be applied. The floor leader transmits this information to the remaining players in the same manner. Care must be taken to give signals at a time when the coach is certain that each player will receive the message. If one player fails to get the instructions, the result can be disastrous.

End of the game. Another strategic use of the pressing defense can be found in end-of-game situations. We always try to prevent our opponent from controlling the play of the game. This is especially true at the end of the game and at the end of the half. This seems an ideal time to bring into play your all-out defensive push. For example—if a team has possession of the ball near the end of the half, invariably they will hold for one shot. This is a stratagem which, to me, has questionable value at best. Nevertheless, it occurs often. If a team is going to take one shot, then it seems logical that the defense can assume greater risks in their efforts to gain possession knowing that the opponent is unlikely to shoot anyway.

In situations like these we often jump into the zone press defense at half-court. We have found that it has changed the complexion of many games at the half. On one occasion our opponent held a six-point lead with a minute and a half to go and attempted to hold the ball for one shot. We went into the zone press and by quick breaks were able to get two field goals while our opponent was unable to score. Having reduced their advantage to two points, we went on to win the game in the second half.

The end-of-game situation offers an equally sound basis for using the zone press. Players intent on maintaining possession of the ball for that last second shot with the score tied are susceptible to all-out pressing tactics. We have been fortunate to win several games when our opponent had possession of the ball, and gone on to score ourselves. Incidentally, we also lost a very vital game to West Virginia in the N.C.A.A. playoffs when we attempted to get a last second shot; our opponent pressured us and came up with a key steal and field goal.

Another strategic use of the man-to-man press is when your team has a one- or two-point lead with very little time (less than 15 seconds) remaining, and the opponent is in possession in his back-court. In situations like this, the opponent is faced with a limiting time factor. If the defense can force the opponent to use a significant portion of this time with a confining, *no foul* press, it will enhance its chances of winning.

Last-ditch effort. Of course the most obvious time to resort to the pressing defense is when your team is many points behind and time begins to run short. This isn't as much a matter of strategy as it is of necessity. There comes a time in every ball game when the coach of the team that is behind can say to himself, "if we don't start pressing now, we're going to lose this ball game." This point in the game varies according to many factors. The manner in which the leading team is conducting its offense; the size of the deficit your team is attempting to overcome; whether or not your team's offense attack is functioning well; the personal foul situation of your players, and many other factors go into the determination of when to start the last desperation press. There isn't a magic formula that yields the precise moment when this defensive move should be made. The pre-season practice of game situations—"10 points behind, 6 minutes remaining," "5 down, 3 minutes left"—will enable the coach to gauge the proper time to go to the press. The coach has to feel it. Frequent experience in such situations guides the coach in determining the "this is it" time.

When a team reaches this point in the game, it is imperative that the coach let out all the stops in an effort to win. I can never understand the coach who inserts his weakest players when his opponent has a commanding lead late in the game. Some of these games could be won by an all-out effort. There is a great lesson in life for players to learn from such situations. They can't learn it if the coach gives up. I think it is better to lose by 15 or 20 points and have made the big effort to win the game, than to sit idly by and watch your team lose gracefully by five or six points. It is winning or losing that counts, not the margin of defeat.

Summary. The "unexpected" is a great tactic to employ at any part of the game. Watch your opponent carefully. Notice if he seems to have gotten a rhythm of attacking your defense. Then make appropriate changes. Perhaps by changing the manner of applying the defense, or the point of application, the offensive team's efforts will be disrupted sufficiently to allow the defense to gain the advantage that it requires.

It seems very significant that the coach is limited in what he can do with his team offensively to change or to alter the course of a game. However, there is a great deal that he can do defensively to accomplish this objective. The coach who sits on the bench and watches his defense get riddled, then offers such excuses as *"Well, they were really hot,"* or *"You can't do much against shooting like that,"* or *"They were too big for us,"*— has done little to warrant the title of coach. Defensive change is the key. The team must be prepared to go quickly and effectively into a variety of defensive techniques. We feel that most of these techniques can be applied from the man-to-man.

We like to keep the zone press in reserve for emergency use. The combination of the two has bailed us out of many a difficult situation. One defense sets up the other. We have had experience of having our opponent lulled into a false sense of security by feeling it has beaten our zone press, when actually we were pressing man-to-man. Then, when we came back with our zone press in the later stages of the game, we were able to disrupt the kind of attack they had been utilizing in the earlier period.

The same thing has happened when we started with the zone press. Teams which have been carefully coached will often find openings that exist in a defense which sends two men after the ball with each pass. But very often players find difficulty in adjusting to the changes required in going from one kind of pressing attack to another. This is really where the games are won. This is where the coach can help his team to win the close ones and to claim the big upset victories.

COACHING TIPS

1. Discover during practice and scrimmage sessions the strength of your press and use it accordingly during the games.

2. Try some form of the zone press during the first half of the game. It will give you an idea of the opponent's attack at a time when possible damage may be overcome.
3. Use the zone press if you are having trouble penetrating the opponent's defense.
4. Use the zone press if your opponent wants to hold the ball for one shot before the end of the half or the end of the game.
5. Be ready to adjust the press if the opponent finds consistent scoring openings.
6. Counteract an opponent's press with one of your own.
7. *Never* assume defeat. Use every defensive tactic at your disposal to help your team win the game.
8. Zone press the team which relies on one or even two good ball handlers to advance the ball. By forcing the other players to handle the ball, the pressing team may be able to benefit from many ball-handling errors.
9. Full-court press the team which is poorly conditioned or shallow in bench strength. Use of the press for extended periods of time will eventually pay dividends.
10. Zone press the inexperienced team.
11. Zone press to spark your own offense when it seems to be lagging.
12. Press the team rallying against your second half lead.
13. Apply moderate no-foul court pressure to the opponent when your team is leading by one or two points with only seconds remaining.
14. Zone press the team with an overwhelming height advantage.

CHAPTER 7

The Standard Zone Defenses

Regardless of a team's primary defense, it should prepare some alternate defense prior to the beginning of each season. At St. Joseph's, we work on two types of the standard zone defense to use on occasion during the course of a season. In recent years we have used the standard zone very sparingly. I do feel, however, that the use of the zone for brief periods of particular games has helped us gain important victories. Our use of the zone, therefore, is dictated by strategic motives.

Strategic use of the zone defense. There are many situations which arise during the course of a game in which the straight or standard zone may be used to advantage. In one game of a recent season, we went into the 1-2-2 zone in the last minute and a half after playing the entire game to that point in our pressing man-to-man. The situation which called for this change was this: Our opponent had obtained possession of the ball with a minute and a half remaining. They trailed by one point, and immediately called time-out. Naturally, they were going to set up an offensive play by which they hoped to obtain the lead. By switching into the zone, we hoped to disrupt their planned attack. It worked. We got possession without the opponent taking a shot and called time-out. I had originally intended to stay in the zone for just that one sequence, but when our players came to the bench they said, "Let's stay in it. They don't know what to do." I went along with the players' suggestion and we stayed in the zone. We won the game by four points.

We have also received great assistance from the zone by shifting back and forth from it to man-to-man. I can think of another situation in which we played nip-and-tuck with an opponent well into the second half. We went into a zone defense with about seven minutes left and managed to score two fast-break field goals. Our opponent called time-out. During the time-out, we changed our defense back to the man-to-man—but just for the next offensive play by our opponent, then we returned to the zone. Our opponent didn't score against the man-to-man and the next time up-court, was confronted with the zone again. After two more scoreless attempts, they called another time-out. This time we went back to the man-to-man, completed the game with that defense, and eventually won by more than 10 points.

There is a generalization that can be made from the above illustrations: It is often helpful to switch to a secondary defense—*even though it may not be as strong as the regularly employed defense*—to catch the opponent off-stride. Ken Loeffler, the former LaSalle College and Texas A & M coach, once remarked that his national championship teams at LaSalle employed what he considered a rather weak zone defense, but it pulled them through many a tight situation because it necessitated a change in attack by the opposition. While the opponent made the adjustment, Coach Loeffler's team was able to secure winning leads.

Teams acquire a certain offensive rhythm during the course of a game. A change in defense will do much to break that performance. This may be done by shifting the point at which one picks up his opponent in his man-to-man; it may be accomplished by jumping into the zone press for brief periods; but it also may be achieved by slipping in and out of the standard zone defense.

The zone defenses we utilize are the 1-2-2 and the 1-3-1 zones. The shifts as we practice them are described here.

1-2-2 ZONE

This zone became popular in the 1955–56 season, the first year that the rules changed the width of the foul lane from six to twelve feet. Although the 1-2-2 is vulnerable in the middle, the amount of time an offensive player can remain in the area below the foul line is limited. This zone alignment covers the sides and corners quite well and affords reasonably good rebounding protection.

Shifts. The shifts required in the 1-2-2 are illustrated by the accompanying diagrams. *Diagram 25* shows the basic alignment into which the team falls as it hustles into defensive position. Since the most vulnerable area is the foul lane, wingmen No. 2 and No. 3 are in tight along the lane, and deep men No. 4 and No. 5 are well up into the lane. This ap-

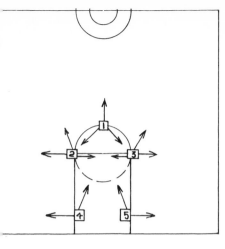

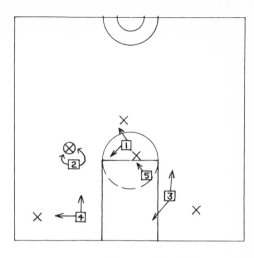

Diagram No. **25**   Diagram No. **26**

pearance will discourage the initial pass from being made into the lane area even if there is a high post-man waiting. We don't want that first pass to enter the lane area under any circumstances.

With the ball on the right shoulder position (*Diagram 26*), the No. 2 man moves aggressively to the ball. Care must be exercised so that the offensive player is not able to drive past the defender and into the heart of the zone. So, while the defenders are encouraged to be aggressive in their attack on any man with the ball in their responsible area of the court, they are cautioned to treat him as a man-to-man opponent if he starts to drive. We want to avoid the wild "lunge-and-hope-for-the-best" kind of defense. Also note in *Diagram 26*, No. 5 has moved deep into the lane and is ready to cover anyone on the post position. No. 4 has edged slightly toward the right corner to cover that area if the next pass is made there.

Diagram No. **27**   Diagram No. **28**

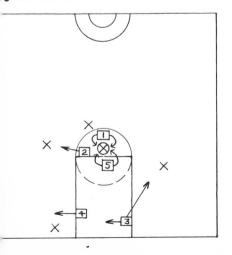

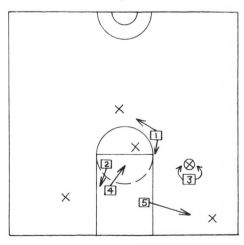

Diagram 27 (*see page 87*) illustrates the shift if the succeeding pass is made to the high post. No. 5 is up on the man on the line, No. 3 has dropped back to protect the under-the-basket area, and No. 1 and No. 2 have turned to face and harass the man with the ball. If the high post-man succeeds in getting the ball to the left shoulder (*Diagram 28*), No. 3 comes quickly to cover the ball and No. 5 returns to the deep position.

If the ball moves into the corner position (*Diagram 29, below*), No. 5 covers there, while No. 4 moves to cover the deep post position. No 4 should, if possible, play in front of any offensive man trying for deep post position. No 3 must overplay the outlet pass. If the players employ the proper shifts they should be in excellent "stealing" position when the ball gets to the corner.

In *Diagram 30* (*see below*) the ball has reached the deep post-man. No. 5 turns and faces the ball, actually doubling-up with No. 4. No. 3 continues to close off the passing lane, while No. 2 covers under the basket.

Diagram No. **29**

Diagram No. **30**

COACHING TIPS ON THE 1-2-2 ZONE

1. Keep the ball out of the lane area.
2. Play deep men (No. 4 and No. 5) well up into lane area.
3. Wingman (No. 2 or No. 3) must shift to cover under the basket if the deep man on the same side moves to cover the lane area. Use the better rebounding wingman in the No. 3 position.
4. Wingmen overplay passing lanes when the ball is in front or in corner.
5. Foul lane is blocked when shot is taken to prevent rebound field goal.
6. Point man (No. 1) drops back to prevent ball from entering lane area from shoulder positions.
7. Play zone aggressively, and don't permit opponent to penetrate zone on the drive.

1-3-1 Zone Defense

The 1-3-1 zone lends itself very readily to the 3-1-1 zone press. The shifts required in each are quite similar. The principal difference is that there isn't the emphasis on doubling-up on the ball in the 1-3-1 that exists in the pressing defense.

The similarity between the two defenses reduces the amount of learning that takes place and makes for relatively easy application.

Shifts. *Diagram 31* shows the 1-3-1 as it sets up. The No. 1 man covers the width of the lane at the top of the circle. Wingmen No. 2 and No. 3 overplay the passing lanes so that the ball may not penetrate to the baseline with one pass. No. 4 protects the lane area and No. 5 guards the hoop.

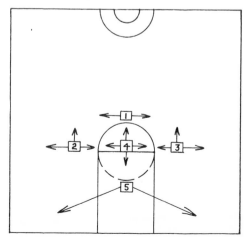

Diagram No. **31**

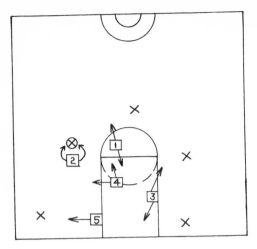

Diagram No. 32

With the ball at the right shoulder position (*Diagram 32*), No. 2 moves out to cover, again striving to close off the passing lane to the baseline. It is important that the wingmen do not advance beyond an imaginary line tangent to the top of the circle. No. 5 has edged toward the right corner; No. 3 protects under the hoop; No. 4 clogs the lane, and No. 1 overplays the passing lane across court.

Diagram 33 (*see below*) shows the ball in the high post position. No. 5 has returned to basket position; No. 3 moves up to cover the left shoulder area; No. 4 plays the ball hard; No. 1 and No. 2 overplay the passing lanes. No. 1, No. 2, and No. 3 are all facing the ball in their attempts to deflect the pass. The wingmen must overplay the passing lanes to the baseline so that the high post-man will have difficulty getting the ball to that vulnerable position.

Diagram No. 33

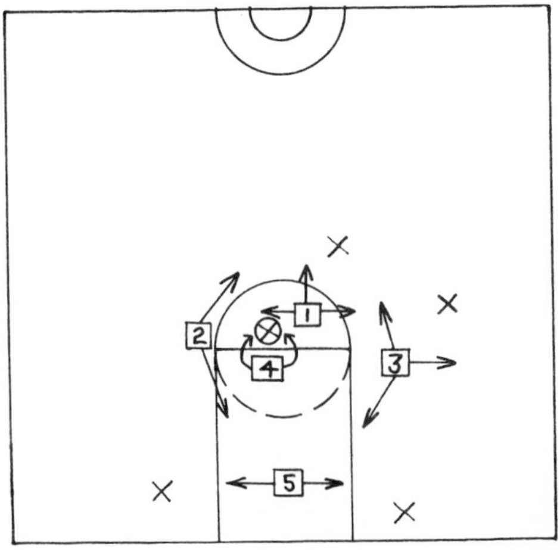

 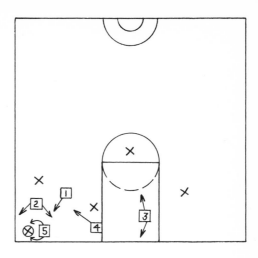

Diagram No. 34   Diagram No. 35

As the ball reaches the baseline (*Diagram 34*), No. 5 moves out quickly; No. 3 covers under the basket, and No. 2 overplays the passing lane out.

With the ball in the corner (*Diagram 35*), No. 5 continues out to that point; No. 4 covers the deep post (from the front, if possible), while No. 3 protects underneath.

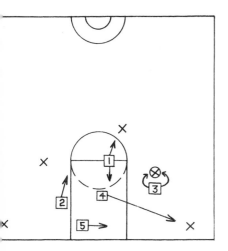

Diagram No. 36

If the ball is passed cross-court (*Diagram 36*), No. 3 moves out quickly as the other players shift back to their original alignment. On cross-court passes, No. 4 has the responsibility of covering the opposite corner.

91

COACHING TIPS ON THE 1-3-1 ZONE

1. Wingmen overplay passing lanes to baseline from the front and to the front area from the baseline.
2. No. 4 should be your best rebounder.
3. No. 5 should be fast and agile since he must cover both corners on most occasions.
4. No. 1 must be quick and alert to harass the opposition out front and to cover the area above the foul line.
5. Wingmen should be adept rebounders since they shift to under-the-basket position when the ball is in opposite corner. Use the better rebounding wingman in the No. 3 position.

TEACHING THE ZONE DEFENSE

It is imperative that the players become thoroughly familiar with their responsibilities in the zone defense and are able to adjust quickly to the demands of this defense in the game situation. After the coach decides which zone defense(s) he will use, he must explain the purpose of the defense and the required shifts to the squad. This explanation is one of detail— dwelling on the individual and team responsibilities and movements. It is a good practice to *ditto* this information and distribute it among the squad members. The use of the magnetic or chalk board will assist the coach in making this information more impressive. Game films illustrating the desired defense are also of great value.

Once the basic information has been digested, the team goes to the floor and walks through the various shifts. Again the coach stresses the individual and team responsibilities—emphasizing which passing lanes he wants to cut off, rebounding responsibilities, fast-break outlets, and any other factors which he deems important. Then the first team works on defense at half-court as the coach directs the attack of the offensive team to cover all of the shift possibilities. The coach attends to the same defense techniques (proper approach to the man with the ball, footwork, blocking out, protecting the baseline, use of hands, overplaying, and sloughing off from the weak side) in teaching the zone as with the man-to-man defense.

As the first team members gain skill and awareness of their zone duties, the coach inserts members of his second unit into the defensive team so that all personnel are familiar with zone requirements.

The next step is to scrimmage with the zone defense under full-court game conditions. The coach may have both teams in the zone defense or one in man-to-man and the other in the zone. In either event, the players should experience enough practice with the defense to be thoroughly familiar with all its demands and they should be capable of moving quickly and efficiently into this formation.

The procedure described permits the coach to practice his zone offense while perfecting the defensive moves of the zone defense.

COACHING TIPS ON GENERAL USE OF ZONE DEFENSE

1. Use a zone defense to change the pace of your opponents' attack.
2. Use a zone defense to initiate fast-break attacks.
3. Use a zone defense to protect a player in personal foul trouble.
4. Use a zone defense to offset "special" play of opponent (especially at the end of the game).
5. Use a zone defense to thwart a driving offensive attack.
6. Use a zone defense against a weak outside shooting team (if you can find one).

CHAPTER 8

Defensive

Practice Sessions

Emphasis. If defense is to be the heart of your game, it is necessary to establish this attitude among the players from the first day of practice. Defense must receive priority in the details of practice. One can't verbally stress defense, then devote all the practice time to the offensive aspect of the game. (Refer to "COACHING TIPS," on pages 26 and 46 for techniques of developing the team's "defensive attitude.")

Planning. Practices must be carefully planned, so that all of the factors which require attention receive the time and effort they need. The coach should carefully organize the available practice time. He should make out a schedule for his pre-season practice prior to its beginning. He should make further schedules for each week of the season prior to the particular week. These schedules should be posted for the attention of the other coaches on his staff. They should also be posted for the players so they will know what the practice will consist of on a given day. I try to limit formal practice time to a period of one hour and a half. Players seem to perform better and with a great deal more zeal with this time limit than with a more extended one.

A copy of a one-week practice plan for St. Joseph's is offered for the reader's interest. This outline is placed on the bulletin boards of the coaches' and players' locker room. It is accompanied by ditto sheets giving a complete description of the drills to be used. Each practice drill listed on the outline is given a reference number pertaining to the description sheet so that the players know exactly what is expected of them in the various drills.

PRE-SEASON PRACTICE

Objectives

(1) Development of Basic Skills

OFFENSE
    Passing
    Shooting
    Dribbling
    Rebounding

DEFENSE
    Stance
    Movement
    Position

(2) Development of Basic Team Concepts

OFFENSE
    One-on-one
    Two-on-two
    Three-on-three
    Change of direction
    Post play

DEFENSE
    One-on-one
        Pressure
        Check advance
        Steal from dribbler
    Two-on-two
        Hard switch
        Double-up
        Check cutter
        Overplay of pass receiver
    Three-on-three
        Overplay

DEFENSE (*cont.*)
Hedge
Pick up
Two-on-one
Double-up
Three-on-two
Double-up

DAILY SCHEDULE

Monday

Squad Meeting: Explanation of objectives
Drills
- (*1*) Parallel passing lines
- (*2*) Three lane passing
- (*3*) Three line passing
- (*4*) Long pass and dribble
- (*13*) Group shuffle: 2 one-minute drills
- (*14*) One-on-one defensive
- (*15*) Two-on-two defensive

Foul Shooting
Shoot five at each of the side and main
court baskets. Total: 40—count number made.
Drills
- (*5*) Drive-in from six court positions
- (*6*) Jump shot drill as above

Tuesday

Drills
- (*1*) Parallel passing lines
- (*2*) Three lane passing
- (*9*) Five-on-five fast break
- (*13*) Group shuffle: 2 one-minute drills
- (*18*) Hands behind back
- (*14*) One-on-one defensive
- (*15*) Two-on-two defensive
- (*16*) Three-on-three defensive

Foul Shooting
Same as Monday

Drills
- (5) Drive-ins
- (6) Jump shooting
- (10) Rebounding
- (7) Change of direction
- (4) Long pass and dribble

Wednesday

Squad Meeting
Brief evaluation of practice
Suggestions for improvement

Drills
- (13) Group shuffle: 1 two-minute drill
- (18) Hands behind back
- (15) Two-on-two defensive
- (16) Three-on-three defensive

Foul Shooting
Same procedure as previous day

Drills
- (7) Change of direction with defense
- (11) Four-on-four change of direction with defense
- (5) Drive-in with defense
- (6) Jump shot with defense
- (10) Three-on-three rebounding
- (9) Five-on-five fast break

Thursday

Drills
- (1) Parallel passing
- (3) Three line passing
- (13) Group shuffle: 2 one-minute drills
- (5) One-on-one drives with defense
- (8) Post split

Foul Shooting
Same procedure as previous day

Drills
- (16) Three-on-three defensive
- (17) Three-on-two defensive
- (13) Weak side hand-off
- (9) Five-on-five fast break
- (11) Four-on-four change of direction

Friday

Squad Meeting
Evaluation of week's work
Suggestions for improvement
Drills
(*13*) Group shuffle: 1 three-minute drill
(*2*) Three lane passing drill
(*4*) Long pass and dribble
(*15*) Two-on-two defensive
(*17*) Three-on-two defensive
Foul Shooting
Same procedure as previous day
(*5*) Drive-in with defense
(*9*) Five-on-five fast break
(*10*) Three-on-three rebounding
(*12*) Weak side hand-off with defense
(*11*) Four-on-four change of direction

Fundamental emphasis. The pre-season practice period is the time to establish the fundamentals which the players must apply during the heat of the season. Attention to detail at this time will save a great deal of time-consuming correction later on. This is the time to insist on proper stance and movement, to establish the rules of switching, doubling-up, leaving one's man to pick up another, body-checking, blocking out on the defensive backboard, and the myriad other facets of the defensive game. The group and individual drills mentioned in the chapters dealing with individual and team development should be stressed during the pre-season workouts. One-on-one and two-on-two drills, full- and half-court, are ideal for inculcating the players with the skills and attitudes desired by the coach.

Installation of defenses. Pre-season is also the time for the coach to establish the basic defense and the secondary defenses which his team will use during the season. The coach must glean from his previous experience every type of game situation with which he will be confronted during the season and be prepared to react with the required defensive move. His basic defense will, of course, receive first attention. It is impossible to have a half-dozen good defenses. It *is* possible to have *one* good one. It is well to strive for this one positive factor. The secondary defenses do not have to be as strong. They are more for the surprise and strategic factors.

When the time arrives for the opening game, each player and the team as a group should be thoroughly schooled in the fundamentals and team procedures required of the defensive alignments to be used through-out the season. Then, when it is time to use a defensive variation in prepa-ration for an opponent, it is only a matter of polishing the details of this move.

Evaluation of defense. It is possible, even though the coach has made a careful evaluation of his material, that the primary defense of his choice is not effective. This judgment should not be made on the spur of the moment. The coach should reach this decision only after a careful consideration of the objectives of the defense and the ability of his team to fulfill them. He must allow sufficient time for the learning process of each individual and the team as a group to function. If possible, he should have the benefit of scrimmages with outside opponents. He should project and envision the progress of his team during the course of the season. Then, if he feels that his team cannot attain the objectives he had set for them, he must make the necessary adjustments. This is best done during the pre-season period. It *must* be done, however, at any part of the season. This is a very difficult decision for the coach to make. But once he is convinced that his primary defense is not doing the job, he must make that decision and work to install an effective replacement.

GAME PRACTICE

Once the game season is underway, the coach must turn his attention to the preparation for the individual games. This does not mean that he forgets the individual drills and personal attention. It does mean that he devotes less time to this and more to the team aspects of defense. That is why the pre-season period is so important to the individual develop-ment of the player. The coach must get most of his fundamental individual defensive work done at this time. Once the games begin, there isn't time for that kind of emphasis.

Evaluate opponent. In preparing for the individual game, a careful analysis must be made first of the opponent. What are his offensive strengths? What are his offensive weaknesses? What are his defensive strengths and weaknesses? The former must be considered in the light of the primary defense of your team. In order to properly evaluate the op-ponent, the coach should see them play an actual game. It is most de-sirable if he is able to see them play a team whose defensive style is similar to his own. Of course, this is not always possible. Often it is not possible for the coach to see the team play at all. If he cannot see them personally, the coach should have his opponent scouted by someone who is thoroughly familiar with his style of play. The coach should instruct this person as clearly as possible what he wants to find out about this team. We will go into the details of scouting an opponent in Chapter 15.

Meet with the staff. Once this information has been obtained, the coach should digest it with those on his staff (if he has assistants) and invite their comments and suggestions on both defensive and offensive play. The coach should come to a decision on how this team is to be played to best advantage.

Team meeting. The next step is to have a team meeting. During this session, the coach explains to the team *what* he plans to have them do and *why*. It is important for the players to know the reasoning behind the coach's decision. All available teaching aids (magnetic board, previous game films, demonstrations, etc.) are brought into use at this time. Then the coach should ask for suggestions and comments from the players. If the player suggestion has merit, it should be incorporated into the game plan. If the coach feels that the suggestion is without value, he should explain to the player his feeling on the suggestion and the idea is dropped. This procedure gives the players a feeling of joining into the strategic aspect of the game and also avails the coach of a source of information that can be most valuable. Both defensive and offensive plans are made at this meeting.

Floor work. Then the team goes on the floor and walks through the planned defensive moves. The next step is to have the junior varsity or freshman team simulate the attack of the opponent while the varsity plays defense. This can be done at whatever point the defense is to be applied— full-court, three-quarter court, half-court, or at the foul circle. When the defensive team acquires possession of the ball, they ready themselves for the offensive attack, but then give the ball back to the other team and the defensive work starts again. This is continued until the defensive work is satisfactory.

Then the defensive team is given the opportunity to go with the ball and attempt to score when they acquire possession. They may score from the fast break or, if there is no break, they have one offensive series with which to score against the opponent's simulated defense. When they have scored or have lost possession, they start with their defensive work again.

Such a procedure provides proper stress on the defensive aspect of the game and also affords practice in switching quickly to offense and attacking the opponent's defense.

Out-of-bounds formations and jump ball alignments are considered in a similar manner, and careful attention is directed to checking the opponent's formations and movements.

This procedure has proven to be the most expedient and, at the same time, the most thorough manner of preparation for the succession of games during a season. When your team plays two and occasionally three times in a week, time is of the essence. The coach must find a way to get the most done in the least amount of time.

Importance of practice. There are many conflicting maxims on the value of practice. "Practice makes perfect," "A team plays the way it practices," "A poor practice makes for a good game," and the like. Regardless of these sayings, no one will deny the importance of the practice session. It is up to the coach to organize practice so that it is meaningful and alive. Players should be aware of the reasoning behind the drills they do and should share the feeling of their importance. Players appreciate and expect good organization on the part of the coach. Attention to this characteristic will do much to maintain a high degree of efficiency on the practice court. This, in turn, will result in better team performance.

COACHING TIPS

1. Never allow a careless or lazy defensive play to go without correction.
2. Return occasionally to fundamental defensive drills during the course of the season.
3. Simulate game conditions during practice sessions—use officials and timer. Work on realistic situations. *For example:*
   a. seven points behind and four minutes to play, opponent's ball out of bounds.
   b. three points behind and one minute to play, opponent's ball out of bounds.
   c. one point behind, ten seconds to play, jump ball.
   d. tie score, thirty seconds to play, opponent's ball out of bounds.
4. Provide personal, individual attention to players who need special work before formal practice gets underway.
5. Practice all the defensive formations you may need frequently enough to assure proper performance.

PART 2

The Development
of Offense

CHAPTER 9

Relationship of Offense to Defense

Application of philosophy to offense. The coach's philosophy affects all phases of the game. It cannot apply to offense or defense alone. There cannot be one philosophy for one phase of the game and a different philosophy for another. You can't expect players to respond to conflicting philosophies as they pertain to different phases of the game. For instance, it is difficult for me to see the reasoning or consistency behind a coaching technique which calls for an all-out fast-break effort on offense and a passive, relaxed brand of defense. The philosophy influences both aspects of the game and should be consistent for each.

Offensive pressure. Our philosophy of basketball has been described. You have seen how it affects the defense which we employ. Our offensive objectives are very similar. We like to apply the same kind of pressure that was used in our defense to our offense. We want to force our opponent to play our kind of game in every respect. To do this we pressure him on both defense and offense. We want to force our opponent to employ a defense that is most advantageous to us. From our defensive formation we hope to get a good many "easy" field goals. That is, we hope to get a large number of lay-ups and short shots that can be acquired at the end of the fast break. If the fast break is not available, then we look for the quick opening drive, the short jumper off screeners, the turning hook and jump shots in close to the basket, and the goals that result from aggressive rebounding. We want to battle our opponent with everything at our disposal in order to score each time we have the ball. If we fail to score, then we must pick up our defense and go to work again until we have possession once more. The same driving force that motivates our defense provides the foundation for our offense as well.

Contribution of defense to offense. From what has been written, therefore, the two phases of the game—defense and offense—are closely related rather than separate and distinct. We rely on our defense to ignite the offense, to spark us in our drive for the basket, and to force our opponent to commit errors. We also rely on our defense to provide us with fast-break opportunities. We feel that if we can get between five and 10 field goals a game from steals, deflections, and interceptions, our defense has contributed heavily to the effectiveness of our offense.

This cannot be said of the passive defense. Such a defense contributes nothing to the offense. The passive defense is mere token resistance. *Pressure defense,* however, gives a great impetus to the offense.

The coach who considers defense as a foundation of the game has already given careful consideration to the material he has on hand, and he has used these considerations in determining the kind of defense his team will play. Once this is done, the coach is able to relate the contributions of his defense to his offense. We have already described the pressure game. If this is the defense the coach employs, he has made the offensive game much easier for his players and certainly far less complex. Most of the work will be done while playing defense. Many of the field goals the team scores will be the fruits of their defensive labors. Without such defensive help the coach must rely more and more on the offensive abilities of his players. He must rely more and more on set plays, a pattern attack, or some free-lance system in order to get that good shot each time his team comes down the court.

Use of material for offense. Stressing the contribution of pressure defense to the offensive phase of basketball is not to be considered as overlooking or disregarding the importance of establishing a definite offensive attack nor should it be considered underplaying the importance of fitting an offensive attack to the available material. Regardless of the defense which a team employs, the coach must use his personnel efficiently on offense. He must analyze the offensive capabilities of his players in the same manner with which he studied their defensive abilities. (Most coaches do this first, attaching secondary importance to the defensive attributes of the players.)

Let us consider the available personnel in the three categories in which they are most often grouped: the big man, the medium-sized man, and the small man. We will do this without reference to specific size since big, medium, and small are terms relative to the competition in which one is playing. At some levels of college competition, for instance, a player is not big unless he measures 6'7" or taller. At other levels of college ball a 6'4" man may be considered as a big man. At the high school level the range is even greater.

The big man. Good big men are hard to find. There seems, however, to be a growing abundance of tall players. The vast majority of major college teams in the country have at least one player who is 6'6" or taller. More and more of these players are appearing at the high school level. These players need developing. It is the job of the coach to assist this development. This is a real challenge. The big man can make an extremely valuable contribution to the team—both defensively and offensively. The big man is most valuable around the basket where he can put his size to best use. Size in mere inches is not the only factor to consider. The physical strength of the player, his bulk, and his leaping ability are also very important. I have seen 6'3" college players play the big man's role because of their great leaping ability, strength, and finesse around the basket. The big man should develop good offensive moves inside the foul line. He should be able to move left and right, learn to shoot with his back to the basket, using both the hook and the jump shot in either direction. He should learn to drive, to tap, and to acquire the very valuable offensive rebound thrust that results so often in the three-point play.

A coach with one big man will want to use this player inside, whether against the man-to-man or the zone. Two big men may be used in a three-out and two-in attack against any defense or they might even use a tandem 1-3-1 offense with one post man high and the other deep. With three big men on a team, it would be advisable to use a two-out and three-in attack, keeping the big men close to the offensive backboard.

The medium range player. This player must be the most versatile on the squad. He must have the ability to drive in either direction; to shoot the jump shot in close, from the corner, and at the top of the circle; and he must be able to rebound aggressively on both boards. He may be called upon to play in the corner, at side-court, at side post, or perhaps even the deep pivot. Sometimes a medium-sized player must be the big man on his team.

The style of offense best adapted to the medium-sized player is determined by the availability of big men on the squad. If there are big men, the medium-sized player contributes most by playing a corner or side-court position. If he is the big man, he will have to be inside where he can rebound. In either event this player is called upon consistently to display his versatility.

The small man. The small man is usually charged with the responsibility of "floor general." He is the fellow who makes the offense *go.* He sets up the other shooters and keeps the defense honest with his own sniping. He must be a good driver in either direction and shoot an accurate jump shot. The small man will find that a good set shot is a great asset. He is also the man usually called upon to lead the fast break.

With two players of this category, a two-out, three-in attack is the most functional; with three small men, a three-two attack is best, with emphasis on the fast break. Four small men and one big man could work effectively from a high post attack. With five small men the most effective attack would be one in which all five players are constantly moving—perhaps a weaving attack against the man-to-man or a continuity attack against the zone. Players so limited would have to score a great deal from the fast break and from the pressing defense to be able to compete against bigger opponents.

COACHING TIPS

1. Make certain that both the offense and the defense are compatible with the coach's philosophy of basketball.
2. Derive definite offensive advantages from the defense.
3. Use the native offensive abilities of the players.
4. Work with the players to develop their offensive skills.
5. Consider the offensive abilities of the individual players in determining the offensive attack to be used.
6. Weld the individual skills of the players into a team effort.

CHAPTER 10

Individual

Offensive

Development

Requirements of the pressure game. Since the results of a pressure defense are often the lay-up and the short jump shot, then the individual requirements for a team utilizing this kind of defense are somewhat minimized. In the type of game which we play at St. Joseph's, we feel it is essential for all of our players to be able to make the driving lay-up and the short jump shot. We expect our big men to have proficiency around the basket and we want our little men to present a threat from the outside.

There is, therefore, lack of specialization by the offensive players since all must be reasonably well-skilled in the offensive fundamentals of the game. We feel there are *three* basic skills which all players must acquire. These skills are:

1. ball handling—passing, dribbling, and driving for the basket
2. shooting—the lay-up shot; jump shot; the set shot; and a shot with the shooter's back to the basket (hook or turning jump); *foul shot*
3. rebounding

Let us examine each of these skills in some detail.

BALL HANDLING

Ball handling is an essential skill for all players regardless of their position on the team. Although the back-court men have more occasion to exercise this fundamental, skilled performance in this tactic is essential for all players to master.

Passing. Passing the ball properly is a must for all players. The basic pass in the game is the *two-handed chest pass. Figure No. 22* (*a,b,c*) illustrates the proper execution of this pass. The pass is delivered off the fingertips (palms of hands do not touch the ball) as the wrists snap down and away from the passer and the *backs of the hands* face each other. The ball has reverse spin if it is passed properly. This pass is received at chest level. The pass receiver accepts the ball in the same manner with which it was given—with relaxed fingers extended, then yielding slightly to cushion the force of the pass. Coaches should insist at the first practice that each player acquire proper delivery of this pass. With the current emphasis on the zone defense and the fast-break offense, it is essential that all players be able to pass the ball effectively with proper accuracy and range.

Fig. 22, a-c: **Two-Handed Chest Pass**

Fig. 22a   Fig. 22b   Fig. 22c

Fig. 23a

Fig. 23b

Fig. 23, a-c:
**Two-Handed
Bounce Pass**

Fig. 23c

The bounce pass, if delivered with two hands, is passed in the same manner as the chest pass except that it hits the floor about two-thirds of the distance from the passer to the receiver. Again, reverse spin will result from a properly delivered pass. This results in a light, easy to receive pass. This pass is often made with one hand. Players must take care to avoid a "windup" for such delivery which limits its effectiveness. The bounce pass should reach the pass receiver at waist level. (*Figure 23*).

Fig. 23, d-f: **One-Handed Bounce Pass**

Fig. 23d

Fig. 23e

Fig. 23f

The *outlet pass* for the fast break must be delivered quickly and accurately. Ideally, the player takes the ball off the backboard, turns while in the air, and passes off before he hits the floor. It takes a great deal of practice before most rebounders are able to attain this objective. The hook pass, baseball pass, and two-handed overhead pass are effective outlet fast-break passes. (*Figure 24 a-e* illustrates the ideal pass-out play; *see below.*)

Fig. 24a   Fig. 24, a-e: **Rebound Pass-Out**   Fig. 24b

Fig. 24c   Fig. 24d   Fig. 24e

The hand-off pass is required for close exchange of the ball between two offensive players. The ball is passed firmly, but at an easily handled speed, and is received at waist level. This pass is especially useful in post play exchanges and in offenses requiring close screening of players.

If the pass receiver is a step or two from the passer, this pass is thrust lightly forward to the receiver. If the receiver is taking the ball from his teammate as he cuts by him, the ball is laid out for the cutter to take from the hand of the passer.

Dribbling. The second phase of ball handling is dribbling. The dribble, although often used to excess, is an essential skill for the individual to master. Good control of the dribble results from a gentle down-

Fig. 25, a-c: **Dribble Right**   *Fig. 25, d-f:* **Dribble Left**

Fig. 25a

Fig. 25d

Fig. 25b

Fig. 25e

Fig. 25c

Fig. 25f

Fig. 25, g: **Drive**

ward pressure of the fingers and thumb on the ball. The player should not permit the palm or the heel of the hand to touch the ball on the dribble. The dribbler must keep his head up in order to see as much of the court as possible. (*Figure 25 a-f* illustrates the proper method of dribbling with both the right and left hands.)

There are actually two types of dribbling: the *control dribble* and the *speed dribble*. The control dribble is used when the player in possession of the ball is closely guarded by one or more of the defensive team. When using this technique, the dribbler keeps low and protects the ball as much as possible with his body. The speed dribble is used when the dribbler has a clear path to the basket. In order to reach his objective in the minimum amount of time, the dribbler straightens his body position and pushes the ball out in front of him.

The change-of-direction or *"switch dribble"* is another important technique for the dribbler to master. This is achieved by switching hands and changing direction simultaneously in a quick, close-to-the-body transfer of the ball from one hand to the other, thus altering the path of the offensive player, without losing stride. (*See Figure 25 h,i,j,k.*) The *change of pace* (*Figure 25 l-o*) is another valuable tactic for the offensive player to master. This involves a change in the speed of the dribbler often accomplished by a "stutter" move which enables the offensive player to catch the defender off balance.

114

Fig. 25l

25, h-k: **Change of Direction**

Fig. 25h

Fig. 25m

Fig. 25i

Fig. 25n

Fig. 25j

Fig. 25o

Fig. 25k

Fig. 25, l-o: **Change of Pace**

The spin dribble or *reverse dribble* (*Figure 25 p-v*) is used when the dribbler is overplayed on the side of the ball to such a degree that a frontal change of direction move would be dangerous. The dribbler turns his back on his man and pivots away on the foot nearer the defender, dribbling with the *same* hand as he turns (*25 q,r,s*). He continues his dribble with the opposite hand as he completes his change of direction. The dribbler must be careful not to "turn the ball over" on his change of direction and must keep his head up to anticipate the attempt of another defensive team member to steal the ball as he spins.

Driving. A good basketball player drives equally well to the left or right. In order to perform this skill properly, the dribbler must keep the ball away from the defensive man. He must, therefore, possess the ability

Fig. 25, p-v: **Spin Dribble**

Fig. 25p

Fig. 25q

Fig. 25r

Fig. 25s

Fig. 25t

Fig. 25u

Fig. 25v

to control the dribble well with either hand and protect the ball with his body. The driver is in a semi-crouched position and leans slightly into the defensive man with the shoulder and arm nearer the defender helping to protect the ball. (*Refer to Figure 25g*). Once the player has acquired sufficient dribbling speed and ball control in either direction, he should develop a variety of *fakes* to free himself for his drive.

The fake is a quick feint made by the offensive player in which he may use his eyes, head, shoulders, arms, legs, and feet, or merely the ball. Any one or all of these factors may be used simultaneously. The most productive of these, however, are the foot moves. Players must be coached in proper foot moves to insure a good, quick fake and then a long, strong initial step to gain the necessary advantage over the defender. *Figure 26* illustrates a variety of such tactics which the driver can use to get a desired half-step advantage. (*See pages 118 to 122.*)

The cross-over step and *rocker step* moves are good faking techniques. *Figure 26 a-e* illustrates the cross-over step. In this move, the driver steps toward the passer as he receives the ball and then crosses back quickly with the same foot. This move often catches the defensive man leaning toward the passer in anticipation and allows the offensive man full protection of the ball with his body as he drives to the hoop. This move is made to the left and right. Its effectiveness can be improved by faking the drive from the cross-over position and then bursting through

Fig. 26, a-e:
Cross-Over Step

Fig. 26a

Fig. 26b

Fig. 26c   Fig. 26d   Fig. 26e

toward the basket in the direction of the first faking step. (*See Figure 26 f through j.*)

 The rocker step is illustrated in *Figure 26 k-q.* In *Figure 26 k* and *l* we see the offensive player after he receives a pass, faking his step toward

Fig. 26, f-j:
Fake Cross-Over

Fig. 26f

Fig. 26g

Fig. 26h

Fig. 26i

Fig. 26j

the basket as the defensive man retreats. The driver draws back his thrusting foot and brings the ball to shooting position (*26m*). Then he drives forward with the same foot toward the basket (*26 n,o,p*). Note the protection of the ball in *Figure 26 m-q* (*see pages 121-122*).

Smart basketball players vary their rocker step and cross-over step moves with a "no-fake" move. A player using this tactic merely bursts past the defensive man without a fake upon receiving the pass. Sometimes the defensive man will anticipate a fake and relax momentarily, expecting the player with the ball to set himself for some kind of feint. On occasions like this, the driver should burst past the defender without any hesitation whatsoever. By combining these offensive moves and working hard to perfect them, the driver can become a great threat to the defense.

Fig. 26, k-q: **Rocker Step**

Fig. 26k

Fig. 26l

Fig. 26m

Fig. 26n

Fig. 26o

Fig. 26p

Fig. 26q

SHOOTING

The abilities of the individual player to score from the field and from the free throw line are essential to the winning team. No matter how tough the defense is, no matter how well a team handles the ball, it will have a difficult time winning if the players on the team are not adequate shooters.

The lay-up shot. The most fundamental shot in the game of basketball is the short lay-up shot. A good basketball player will be able to make this shot with either hand at the conclusion of his hard drive for the basket. The most important aspect of the lay-up shot is to place the ball softly on the backboard. If a player is successful in driving to the basket, it is not essential that he take off from the proper foot (left foot for the right hand shot, and right foot for the left hand shot). The important factors are to get to the basket on the drive, protect the ball with the body, and lay the ball gently on the backboard. Players driving from the left hand corner may find they are able to afford better protection to the ball by shooting with their right hand. (*See Figure 27 a-e, below.*) This same principle holds for the player driving in from the right side of the basket. The position of the defensive man may be such that it would be to the driver's advantage to lay the ball up with the left hand (*See Figure 27 f,g, and h*). Note strong initial step, ball protection, head-up position of driver in each sequence.

Fig. 27a   Fig. 27, a-i: **Lay-Up Shot**   Fig. 27b

Fig. 27c   Fig. 27d   Fig. 27e

The size of the player is a determining factor in whether the driver will lay the ball up in an underhand or an overhand motion. *Figure 27i* shows the driver laying the ball up unmolested in an underhand lay-up. Generally speaking, the small man finds greater success in laying the ball up with an underhand delivery rather than an overhand one. He is able to get the shot off better against the taller defensive men who may be in the lay-up shooting area. The big man, however, generally has greater success if he leaps high in the air and lays the ball up on the board. (Refer again to *Figure 27 a-h*.)

Fig. 27f   Fig. 27g   Fig. 27h

The player who uses the underhand lay-up technique must lay a "dead ball" on the backboard rather than one with excessive top spin. The latter shot continues to rise after it hits the board and results in many missed attempts. The ball without overspin will drop downward into the basket.

All players must achieve a high degree of efficiency with the lay-up shot. Contrary to common belief, the lay-up shot, when it comes on the end of a drive, is not an easy shot to make. The driver is fighting at least one defensive man. It takes great skill to maneuver into the scoring area and, with good body control, to lay that ball up gently on the backboard

Fig. 27i

for a scoring play. The coach must devote ample practice time to this—the most basic aspect of the offensive game. Concentration on the basket by the lay-up shooter just prior to the moment of release will greatly improve his accuracy. Often a shooter becomes so concerned about his shot getting blocked or looking for an open man, he jabs his lay-up in the general direction of the basket only to find the ball roll off the rim. Concentration is vital.

The jump shot. Most coaches feel that the jump shot has revolutionized the offensive phase of basketball. It is a shot which many feel is indefensible. Players have achieved great accuracy at exceptional ranges with this shot. It is truly a devastating offensive weapon.

Fig. 28a   Fig. 28b

Fig. 28, a-o: **Jump Shot**

The jump shot, like the lay-up, may be delivered in a number of ways. It may be shot at the peak of the shooter's leap—with shooting arm fully extended over his head. (*See Figures 28 a and b.*) Using this technique the shooter relies on his leaping ability to get up over the defensive man. Another technique is to shoot the ball quickly with hardly any jump at all. (*See Figures 28 c,d, and e.*) In this technique the shooter is relying on the unexpected, quick move to get the shot off before the defensive man is prepared to stop him. Once again the size of the player is important. The smaller man who usually plays the outside or in the corner will find that he needs a quick move to get his shot off. *Figure 28 f-h* (*see page 128*) illustrates this move. The driver, noting the defender falling back, stops short, *squares his position to the basket* and shoots his jumper. For this type player, a quick jump shot is very effective. For the big man who is shooting closer to the basket and who is usually confronted by taller defensive opposition, the leaping jump shot is required. Of course, the range of the shooter diminishes with the height of his leap. Many jump shooters can shoot with great accuracy from a distance beyond the top of the circle with the quick shot technique. There are very few who are able to use the leaping jump shot from a position deeper than the top of the circle.

Fig. 28c

Fig. 28d

Fig. 28e

Fig. 28f

Fig. 28g

Fig. 28h

Regardless of the technique employed, the shooting principles remain the same. The ball is shot off the fingertips of the shooting hand. The remaining hand acts as a guide to help position the ball. As the shooter readies himself for release, the guiding hand is removed. In teaching this shot the coach should insist that the elbow of the shooting arm remains perpendicular to the floor and that the shooter effects an exaggerated follow-through until the player has acquired proper technique and accuracy. With this follow-through, the wrist snaps forward and the extended fingers point in the direction of the basket. (Refer again to *Figure 28 b and d.*)

Another jump shooting technique is illustrated in *Figure 28 i-n.* This particular tactic is a valuable acquisition for the post-man. In the illustration the post-man receives the pass with his back to the basket, gives a short head and ball fake to his right and then wheels quickly to his left, using the left foot as his pivot foot. He faces the defender and jumps and shoots all in one motion. The final picture shows the shooter ready to drive toward the basket for the possible rebound. As with the outside jump shooter, the height of the player as well as his leaping ability has much to do with the technique employed in the jump shot. If the post-man is able to use his height and leaping ability to get up over the defensive man consistently, then it is to his advantage to shoot his jumper from the highest point possible. If, on the other hand, the shooter lacks these qualities, then he may have to rely on a quick move. The shooter in the illustration (*Figure 28 i-n*) is 6'5". He is shooting against a 6'8" defender. Although he shoots the ball from a high position, the entire move takes place

Fig. 28i   Fig. 28j   Fig. 28k

Fig. 28l   Fig. 28m   Fig. 28n

very quickly. The shooter attempts to get the play completed before the defensive man has proper time to react. *Figure 28o* shows this maneuver in the game situation. Note that the shooter is up and ready to shoot before the defender reacts to his move.

The post-man who includes the turning jump shot with his drive in either direction and a good hook shot is an extremely tough man to defense. The post-man will find that he is able to complete a variety of moves successfully by turning and facing the defensive man from the high post position. From this point he can jump-shoot, or drive for the lay-up or hook shot with equal facility. The cross-over and rocker steps are excellent for this situation.

The set shot. Although the set shot is used less frequently than in the past because of the popularity and range and accuracy of the jump shot, there is still a definite place for this weapon in the offensive repertoire of the player. The set shot may be delivered with either one hand or two. *Figure 29 a-d (see next page)* shows the two-handed technique. Note how the shooter fakes a step as if to drive, then, as he returns to shooting position, he keeps the ball high and follows through freely. In teaching this

Fig. 28o

Fig. 29, a-h: **Set Shot**

Fig. 29a   Fig. 29b   Fig. 29c   Fig. 29d

shot, the coach makes sure that the shooter keeps the palms and the heels of his hands off the ball. The ball is held lightly with the fingers and thumbs. The two-handed shot is released in the same manner as the two-handed pass. The hands turn out and away and the backs of the hands turn toward each other. Unrestricted follow-through of the body is essential for proper delivery of this shot.

The one-handed set shot (*Figure 29 e-h*) (*see below*) is delivered in much the same way as the two-handed shot except that the free hand helps to control the ball until it is in final shooting position. As with the two-handed shot and the jump shot, the follow-through of the hand, arm, and body is essential.

The set shot should be executed from a range comfortable for the player. He should be able to shoot this shot from a step beyond the foul circle without straining. When a player is so far from the basket that he must exert himself to reach the hoop, then he is beyond a good percentage shooting distance.

Fig. 29e

Fig. 29f

Fig. 29g

Fig. 29h

The hook shot. The hook shot is taken from a back-to-the-basket initial position of the shooter. *Figure 30 a-c* illustrates this move. Upon receiving a pass, the post-man gives a quick body fake to his right and then pivots on his left foot, looking at the basket as he turns. He then sweeps the shot with his shooting arm fully extended and his other arm protecting the ball against the defensive man.

Notice that he is turning into the basket so that he will be able to follow up. A good post man makes this move with either hand from either side of the basket. *Figure 30d* shows the hook shot taken in the game situation. Note how the shooter protects the ball with his body while turning to the basket.

Fig. 30a

Fig. 30b

Fig. 30, a-d: **Hook Shot**

Fig. 30c

Fig. 30d

FOUL SHOOTING

Importance. Accuracy at the free throw line is another factor in the make-up of the successful basketball team. Countless games are decided each year at the 15-foot marker. A team that consistently makes the tough, pressure-packed foul shots at the end of the game wins a high percentage of the close ones. The team that lacks this ability finds that late game leads evaporate as the trailing team takes advantage of scoring opportunities while holding its opponent to non-productive free throw attempts.

Delivery. It has been my experience that players shoot free throws most accurately by using the same technique as with their outside shot. Since most players shoot the one-handed set and jump shots, most shoot the one-handed free throw. Those few who shoot the two-handed set shot, often use that same delivery from the foul line. In my coaching experience at St. Joseph's, close to 95 percent of the players have shot their free throws with one hand. (They established a 73 percent norm of successful completions.)

Those players who are not successful with the one- or two-handed set shot delivery of the free throw (the standard required for success depends upon the level of competition) should be induced to shoot by the two-handed, underhand method. This method has declined in popularity since the era when coaches demanded that each player shoot his fouls in that manner. Nevertheless, some players find this to be an excellent shooting technique.

Technique. Regardless of the style of delivery, successful foul shooting hinges on three factors:

1. Proper shooting form
2. The poised but relaxed temperament of the shooter
3. Complete concentration on the task of shooting

Proper shooting form is acquired by devoting ample practice to the technique employed in the delivery of the free throw. The form of the one- and two-handed set shooters must be carefully checked to assure the consistently well-delivered shot from the foul line. The same principles apply for these shooters in this shot as in their shooting from the field. Most good outside shooters—either jump or set—are consistently high percentage free throw shooters.

Those players who have not acquired a good outside shot, or who cannot master the one- or two-handed set shot from the free throw line, should adopt the two-handed, underhand technique of shooting. This method is illustrated in *Figure 32*. The ball is held lightly with the fingers and the arms are fully extended prior to initiating the shot (*32a*). With a slight bend of the knees, back and arms straight (*32b*), the shooter imparts a slight reverse spin to the ball as he lofts it toward the basket (*32c*). The arms follow through over the shooter's head after the release of the ball (*32d*). This technique results in a "soft" shot which will often drop in the basket even though it may not be quite "true."

Shooting drill. After the shooters have acquired a reasonable degree of success in their particular styles of shooting, the coach works on the second and third factors in successful foul shooting. A method used at

Fig. 32a   Fig. 32b   Fig. 32c   Fig. 32d

Fig. 32, a-d: **Foul Shooting**

St. Joseph's to instill poise and confidence in the shooters is to simulate a one-and-one situation in which each player takes his turn for a possible two shots. After each player has had an opportunity at the one-and-one, the procedure is repeated until each player has used his number of potential attempts. The coach may set this number at 10, 20, 30 or any number he wishes. I have found that 10 possible scores puts the most pressure on the players.

This drill makes each free throw important and moves the shooter off the line after a maximum of two shots. Both of these factors are in keeping with the game situation. The coach may divide his squad into two groups to bring competition into the drill. The same procedure is followed as described above. The greater aggregate number of successful free throws marks the winning team. This provides good pressure foul shooting practice and, at the same time, stimulates interest in a sometimes perfunctory chore.

COACHING TIPS ON FREE THROW SHOOTING

1. Let the players select their own technique of shooting.
2. Work with them to improve their form of delivery.
3. Allow the player a good chance to succeed with his method.
4. If successful, don't change a player's technique of shooting.
5. Simulate pressure situations during practice sessions.
6. When changing a player's style of shooting, establish good habits to assure proper delivery in the new method.
7. Acknowledge the excellent free throw shooter.
8. Use good free throw shooters in the end of the game situations when possible.
9. Use the best pressure foul shooter for technical foul situations.

OFFENSIVE REBOUNDING

Offensive rebounding may be divided into two classifications: the *tip-in* and the *offensive thrust*. Each has a definite place in the rebounding technique of the player.

Fig. 31, a-d: **Offensive Rebound**

Fig. 31a   Fig. 31b   Fig. 31c   Fig. 31d

The tip-in. The tip-in is used by the offensive player who is able to out-position his opponent, get up high, extend his arm fully, and tap the ball with his fingertips directly into the basket or off the backboard into the basket. This tactic is limited to rebounds in the immediate vicinity of the basket. Players should not attempt to slap the ball at the basket. The tap-in is a deft move made with the fingertips. It is a sharp tap at the ball. When the ball is so far from the hoop that the rebounder is unable to tap the ball properly, he should catch the ball, return to the floor and ready himself for the next offensive move.

The offensive thrust. The second technique of offensive rebounding is that of the offensive thrust. The rebounder uses this tactic when he has recovered a missed shot beyond the tipping range. This move requires that the offensive rebounder obtain firm possession of the ball and then thrust his body toward the basket while protecting the ball and keeping it in a high position. In *Figure 31,* the rebounder has outmaneuvered the defensive man to obtain possession. He returns to floor position, gives a short, quick head and shoulder fake. Having raised the defensive man, the rebounder then *steps in* and thrusts his body hard to the basket, keeping the ball in a vise-like grip with two hands until just before he releases his shot on the backboard. This is a strong rebounding play and frequently results in the prized three-point play. Rebounding position is essential. It is also hard to obtain against the well-drilled defensive player. The offensive rebounder must jockey for position, learning to roll off the defender's block-out attempt. Good position provides him with a scoring opportunity on any rebound he gets in the vicinity of the offensive backboard. It puts great stress on the defensive player. When the rebounder thrusts to the basket he invites contact with the defensive man, whose instinctive reaction is to jump up and into the rebounder. This generally results in a personal foul by the defensive man at a time when the offensive rebounder is still moving toward the basket and is in a position to shoot the ball. The player who is able to maintain control of the ball on such a move, and take it to the basket in a strong manner, will gather a great many three-point plays during the course of the season.

13 DRILLS ON OFFENSIVE FUNDAMENTALS

The acquisition of the fundamental skills mentioned in this chapter is vital to individual development and the ultimate success of the team. Players acquire these skills through carefully supervised repetition of these fundamentals. It is the purpose of the following drills to provide this practice.

Parallel line passing drill. The passing drill in *Diagram 37, page 140,* shows the squad in parallel lines facing each other starting at the width of the foul lane. Under the careful eye of the coach, the ball is passed to the player opposite the passer then back and forth down the line. The coach checks for proper delivery of the pass. As skill is increased the players step back one pace to increase the distance of the pass. Proper delivery of each

Diagram No. **37**

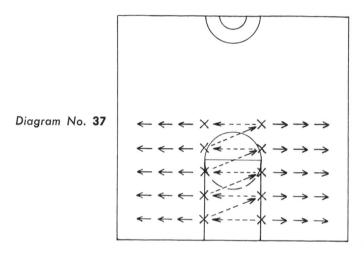

pass is demanded by the coach. Two- and one-handed air and bounce passes may be utilized in this drill.

Man-in-circle passing drill. *Diagram 38* shows one man in the center of a passing circle. The objective of the man in the middle is to get a hand on a pass. The passers attempt to pass by the defensive player without

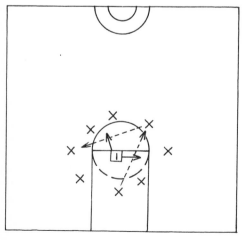

Diagram No. **38**

permitting him to touch the ball. The passer must skip an appropriate number of players on either side (depending on the number of players in the drill) so that proper faking of the pass and sharpness of delivery are assured. If the defensive man touches a pass, he is replaced in the middle by the passer. The drill continues until all players have been in the center.

Three-lane passing drill. This drill, operated on a full-court basis, begins with the squad in three lines at the end of the court. (*See Diagram 39.*) The ball is passed back and forth from the middle man to the wingmen as it is advanced the length of the court. When the passers reach the opposite foul line, the ball is in possession of the middle man who stops and passes to either of the wingmen who goes in for the lay-up. The ball is retrieved by the other wingman who passes out. The three lanes are filled once more and the trio returns to the end of the court using the same scoring technique. Players remain in their passing lanes until they are in the shooting part of the drill. All passes in this drill are two-handed air passes except for the scoring pass which is a bounce pass.

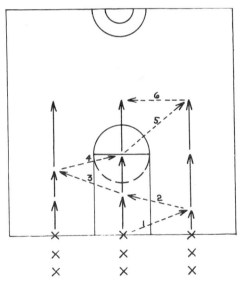

Diagram No. **39**

Three-line passing drill. The drill shown in *Diagram 40* is a variation of the three-lane drill. In this drill the passer cuts behind the pass receiver as they start up-court. This results in a three-man weave and a short pass and hand-off drill. As in the three-lane drill, the ball is advanced full-court until the lay-up is obtained, and then it is returned to the starting end of the court, where another trio of passers takes over.

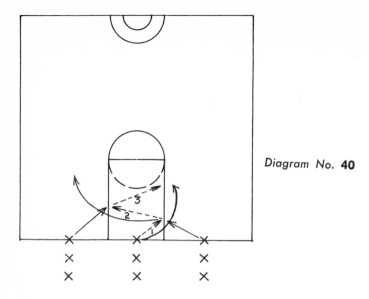

Diagram No. **40**

Split post drill. This drill is a sharp passing drill which also combines the drive for the basket and the lay-up shot. The ball is passed from the guard position to the forward and then to the post-man who breaks out from the baseline to meet the ball. The forward and guard cut off the post-man in that order. The post-man hands off to either one. The pass receiver drives in for the lay-up. The ball is retrieved by the post-man who wheels and throws out to the guard position. Each player then returns to the end of his respective line. It is possible to keep two balls moving in this drill. The drill is worked from either side of the court. (*See Diagram 41, directly below.*)

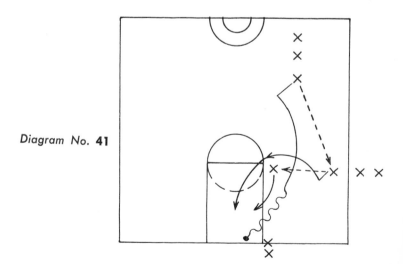

Diagram No. **41**

Change-of-direction passing drill. The purpose of this drill (*Diagram 42*) is to sharpen player movements, especially the change of direction. X1 passes to X2, comes off his back and receives a hand-off pass. X2 moves to the top of the circle, and then sharply breaks down the lane. X1, after receiving X2's hand-off, passes sharply to X3 and cuts off his back. X3 may pass to X2 breaking down the lane or hand off to X1 coming off his back. Whichever player receives the pass drives to the basket and lays the ball in. The player not receiving the hand-off retrieves the ball, passes out to X1 position and each player then rotates one position in a clock-wise direction.

Diagram No. **42**

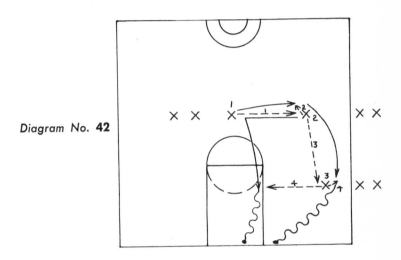

We add defensive players to this drill to obtain realistic practice in a segment of our complete offensive pattern. Along with the ball handling and change-of-direction practice of the guards, this drill also affords an excellent opportunity for the forwards to practice many fundamental skills. Forwards concentrate on breaking out to receive the ball, or if over-played too much, cutting behind the defensive man (backdoor move) to the basket. If the forward comes to meet the pass, we want him to receive the ball with a short, forward straddle-hop with his inside foot extended. This is the foot nearer the foul lane. With this foot forward, he is able to protect the ball, *pivot* on that foot to pass to the cutter through the lane, or *pivot* to hang up X1's man as he drives off. The foot position of the forward is of vital importance, since it determines the effectiveness of his screen, his ability to pass to the free cutter, and his readiness to drive for the basket.

Long pass and dribble drill. The squad is divided in half at either end of the court as in *Diagram 43* (*see below*). A player under the basket dribbles to the side of the lane and throws a hook, baseball, or two-handed chest pass to his cutting teammate. The pass receiver then drives hard to the other end of the court and lays the ball up. The passer then breaks up-court and receives a similar long pass from the next player in line who has retrieved the lay-up. After the driver lays the ball up, he goes to the end of the line at that end of the court and waits his turn to retrieve the lay-up shot and pass up-court to the player in front of him. This drill is worked on either side of the court so that players acquire practice in making a long pass in either direction. This is a good conditioner as well as a drill providing long passing and dribbling practice.

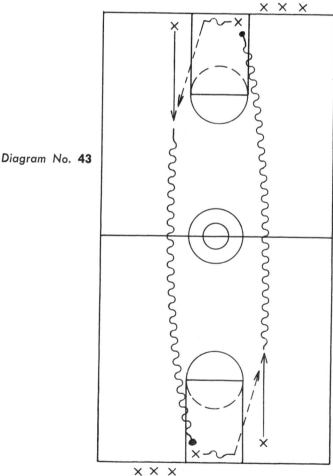

Diagram No. **43**

Diagram No. **44**

Speed dribble relay. (*Diagram 44*). The squad is divided evenly over half-court or full-court. The first players in each line start on a signal by the coach and dribble as rapidly as possible down one side of the line and back the other, handing the ball off to the first man and taking his place in line. The player in possession of the ball then repeats this process until each player has handled the ball. This drill is started first at one side of the line and then the other to assure dribbling practice with either hand. The first team to complete the drill is the winner.

Diagram No. **45**

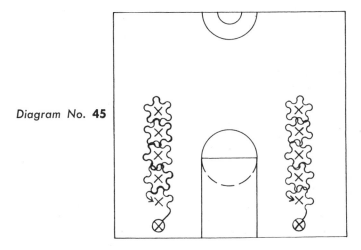

Control dribble relay. This drill (*see Diagram 45, above*), is similar to the previous one. In this drill, however, a dribbler uses a change-of-hands and change-of-direction move to cut sharply in and out among the members of his team. As with the other drill, the first team to have all of its players complete the drill is the winner.

Drive-in drill. This drill affords the player an opportunity to obtain practice in his offensive moves from five positions on the court (A,B,C,D,E). Players take the positions designated in *Diagram 46*. X3 dribbles across and makes his pass to X1 who breaks out to meet the ball.

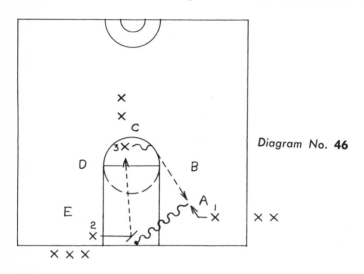

Diagram No. **46**

X1 then executes a cross-over step or a rocker step move and drives the baseline. X2 moves to the lane area and offers token resistance to the driver. X2 retrieves the ball and passes out to the X3 position and players rotate clock-wise one position. Players acquire practice in driving the baseline and through the lane from all five positions lettered in the diagram.

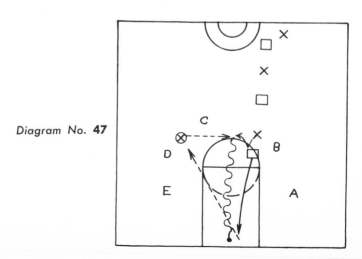

Diagram No. **47**

They also acquire practice with all of the individual offensive moves which they should incorporate into their game.

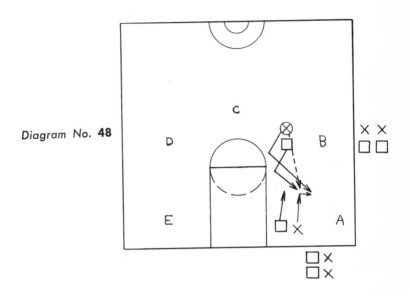

Diagram No. **48**

One-on-one drill. This drill is similar to the drive-in drill except that the driver is now confronted by a defensive man. He receives his pass and uses his fake for whatever kind of good shot he is able to obtain. This drill provides the offensive man with work on his set shot, jump shot, and drive from the five lettered positions designated in *Diagram 47*. As with the other drills, players rotate one position clock-wise at the completion of each series.

Two-on-two (guard-post) drill. *Diagram 48* illustrates a drill for two-man plays off the post. The offensive player makes his pass to the post and then works for whatever play develops. It is possible for him to get the drive-in, the jump shot, and even the set shot. This drill also gives the post-man the same kind of practice in positioning and pivoting (again on the inside foot) mentioned in the description of the change-of-direction drill (*Diagram 42*). The post-man gets shooting practice from the post position and rebounding work against his defender. The drill continues until the offensive team scores or the defensive player recovers; he then passes out sharply to the new team which breaks into position to start its drill.

Rebounding drill. The drill illustrated in *Diagram 49* provides practice in positioning and blocking out defensive positions. The player with the ball at the foul line is permitted to shoot the jump shot above the hand of the defensive man. When the shot is taken, all defenders block out, while the offensive players fight for rebounding position and the offensive rebound. If they are able to score on a tap-in or on the offensive rebounding thrust, then they keep the ball and are allowed another attempt at scoring.

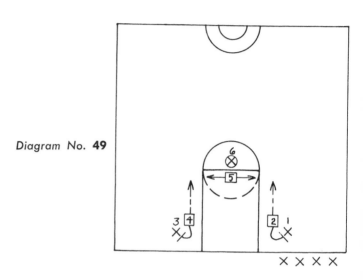

Diagram No. **49**

Once the defensive team has recovered, the pass out is made to the man playing the original shooter as he breaks to the side of the rebound. Players rotate one position at the completion of each drill. A new man takes the X1 position and X6 goes to the end of the line. This drill provides practice in blocking out, offensive board work, passing out and getting into position to receive the outlet pass.

COACHING TIPS

1. Break fundamentals down to components in teaching players.
2. Be meticulous about the quality of execution of fundamental skills.
3. Use a variety of drills.
4. Don't stay in any one drill for an extended period of time.
5. Organize drills so that player rotation is provided.
6. Carefully explain drills to the squad.
7. Explain the purpose of the drills to the squad.
8. Give the drills an identifying name so that the squad responds quickly to the verbal command of the coach.

9. Combine as many skills as possible in each drill.
10. Incorporate your particular offensive and defensive tactics into the drills by developing drills which are segments of the whole pattern (i.e. two-on-two defensive drill, emphasizing switching and doubling-up; change-of-direction drill, stressing ball handling, change of direction, positioning, pivoting, and shooting).
11. Remember—plenty of supervised practice and patience will bring results.

CHAPTER 11

Team
Offense

A team's offense is made up of the group and individual methods by which the team expects to score. A good offense is a careful merging of individual abilities. It provides within the framework of team play an opportunity for each player to utilize his offensive talents to the fullest.

The St. Joseph's pressing defense described in the earlier chapters leads to many fast-break stituations. These are situations in which we equal or outnumber the defensive men in position to meet our quick thrust down-court. We want to take advantage of such opportunities by an organized fast-break attack.

THREE-LANE FAST BREAK

The fast break may be reduced to the four P's:

1. Possession
2. Position
3. Penetration
4. Point production

To obtain top efficiency in the fast break, we drill on each of the above aspects. Then when the parts are assembled, we find the break works with greater effectiveness.

Possession. Possession of the ball leading to the fast break may result from the steal, deflection, interception, rebounding, score by the opponent, and any violation by the opponent by which we get the ball. The methods of obtaining possession through steals, deflections, and interceptions have already been described.

It may be well to emphasize the rebounding aspect of the break. Position is the most pertinent of the tactics involved in rebounding. It is essential to good rebound performance. Once the ball has been obtained, the rebounder must move it out to position where it may be advanced into enemy territory. This is done with a quick pass. Ideally, the rebounder leaps, takes the ball off the board and, while he is in the air, turns and quickly passes to a player up-court. If the rebounder, in turning, sees that he has no immediate outlet, he drives up-court with the ball until he can pass to an open teammate. The rebounding drill, illustrated in *Diagram 49*, provides practice in the offensive and defensive rebound and outlet fast-break pass. (Refer again to *Figure 24, see page 112*.)

Position. Proper position on the break means filling the lanes so the ball is passed to the outlet player, then to the middle position either by passing or dribbling. If the outlet receiver passes the ball, he must make sure that the receiver is coming to meet the ball. This is a must! Many pass interceptions result from the pass receiver breaking up-court to receive the middle pass instead of coming to meet the pass.

The three lanes are filled as soon as the ball gets to the middle position. The two front defensive men (most often the guards) fill one of the wing positions and the middle position. The third position (the other wingman) is filled by the player in the best position to do so. Often this

Diagram No. **50**

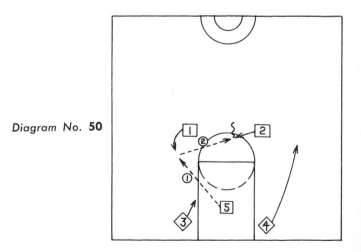

player is a deep defensive man who has not been involved in the rebound. The wingmen are on either side of the middle man, slightly up-court of him, and a short passing distance (about 10 feet) on either side. The first trailer takes position several strides to the rear of the middle man. The second trailer (usually the rebounder) follows the play up-court. He acts as safety man in the event of an opponent's interception. He may also enter the break as a second trailer if the defense has recovered sufficiently to provide four on four opposition. *Diagram 50* shows how the lanes are filled in readiness for the attack on the opponent.

Penetration. The ball is advanced quickly into enemy territory. The safest method of advancing the ball is for the middle man to dribble it. He should not, however, take chances if he is challenged by a defensive man. On such instances he should pass and cut to receive the return pass. If he is unchallenged, he reduces the possibility of interception by advancing the ball on the dribble. The ball stays in the middle position until the middle man reaches the foul line area. Wingmen maintain their position a step or two in advance of him. The team is now ready for the scoring phase of the break.

Point production. When the middle man has reached the foul line, he should quickly evaluate the situation. If no one plays him, he should drive all the way to the basket. If he is met by a defensive man at the foul line, he should find the open player on a three-on-one or three-on-two situation and make his pass. If on a three-on-one, three-on-two, or three-on-three situation the defender keeps hanging back, the middle man should stop in the vicinity of the foul line and take his jump shot. If the same player assumes the vital middle man role consistently, he must be a player with good perception, good deception, and good hands for getting the pass to the open man. He should take pride in the number of scoring plays he can set up, whether he scores himself or provides a scoring assist.

The position of the wingmen is of great importance. Once they have reached a position at the foul line extended, they make a diagonal cut to the basket. This is a wide angle cut in which the wingmen approach the baseline and come into the basket from that point. Such a move provides a good target for the middle man's scoring bounce pass. The cutter receiving the pass drives to the basket. The middle man holds position momentarily at the foul line after making his pass. If the pass receiver is covered, he will often find the middle man open for an outlet and the short jump shot. If the defense has created a three-on-three situation, then the middle man must clear the foul lane so that the first trailer can come through. He may clear this position by dribbling over to the side and then passing to the trailer or he may pass to one of the wingmen and cut through to the opposite side-court. If the defense is able to match four-on-four,

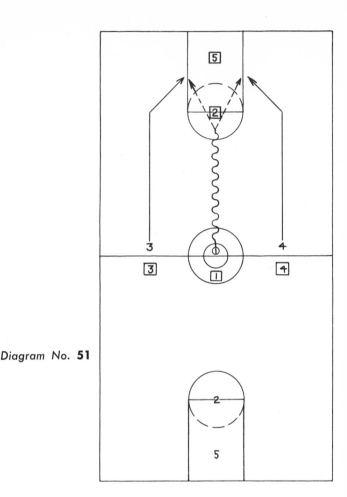

Diagram No. 51

then the second trailer comes through the cleared lane area and the original middle man moves to the back-court for defensive balance.

Fast-break drill. *Diagram 51* illustrates a drill for realistic fast-break practice. This is a five-on-five drill which provides work with both the offensive and defensive aspects of the break. It provides continuous fast-break experience for 10 players. The coach may also incorporate pressing defensive tactics on the two offensive men since, when they recover the ball, there is a double-up opportunity in constant progress.

COACHING TIPS ON THE FAST BREAK

1. Analyze material to determine whether the team is capable of operating an efficient fast break.

2. In analyzing material consider speed, ball-handling ability, rebounding strength, and most important of all, the ability of the middle man to handle the ball well in making the scoring play on the break.
3. Drill on the four aspects of the break individually so that maximum efficiency in each is attained.
4. Never allow team to force the fast break—but at the same time take advantage of all three-on-one, three-on-two, and three-on-three situations when they present a good opportunity to score.
5. Make use of the five-on-five drill to firm up proper techniques and to establish good habits operative in the fast break.
6. If the fast-break situations are not reaching expected point production, limit their use so that your team at least has possession of the ball and can operate its regular offensive pattern.
7. The effective fast break requires well-conditioned personnel capable of sustained offensive and defensive effort. Practices must be geared to build stamina as well as the necessary skills.

ST. JOSEPH'S MULTIPLE MAN-TO-MAN OFFENSE

If there is no fast-break opportunity, or if the opportunity seems to be of questionable value, then the team should set up in its regular offensive formation. In recent seasons we have used a two-three, high and low post offensive attack. The initial lineup of this offense is illustrated in *Diagram 52*.

Numbers 1 and 2 are the back-court men, 3 and 4 the front-court men, and 5 the post-man. The diagram shows the front-court men a step inside

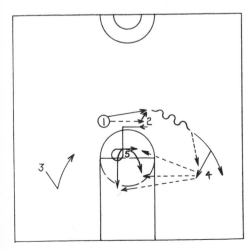

Diagram No. **52**

the foul line extended and several paces inside the side line. The post-man faces the ball in the back-court. No. 1 passes to 2, cuts off his back and receives the return pass, and dribbles over until he has a clear passing lane to front-court man 4. After 2 hands off, he moves across the court to a position at the top of the circle then, timing his move, runs his man off 5. The latter has turned and faces the basket, providing a broad base and back to help 2 hang his man up. No. 2 may run his man off either side of the post or he can run him inside and then dart back to get a jump shot using 5 as a screen.

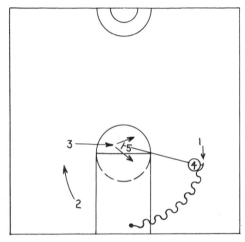

Diagram No. **53**

If 2 goes through and does not receive a pass, he clears out away from the ball and 1 drives either to the front or back of 4 for a hand-off. (*Diagram 53.*) If 1 has an advantage over his man, he should drive to the basket.

If 1 is checked, 4 rolls back and sets a double screen alongside 5—the opposite front-court man (3) who breaks to the foul line position (*Diagram 54*). Both 4 and 5 are facing the basket as they set their screen ready to cut to the basket if the defense gets caught in a switching error. If both defensive men stay with 4 and 5, 3 runs his man either in front or in back of the screeners. By coming in back he ofen frees himself for a jumper. By driving in front he may be able to hang his man on the screen and break down the lane for the easy lay-up. If neither 3 nor 4 is open, they clear out to opposite sides and 1 is free to work off the high post individually (*Diagram 55*); also, he may run a two-man split off the high

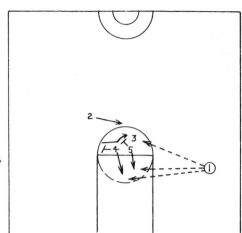

Diagram No. **54**

Diagram No. **55**

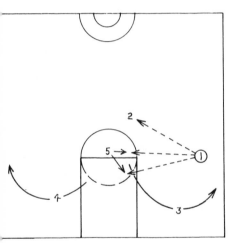

Diagram No. **56**

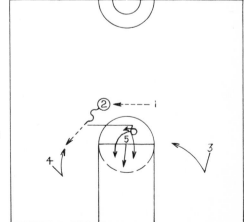

post with 2 who has returned to the back-court position. If this sequence does not produce a good shot, then the offensive players are in position to run the same pattern to the opposite side (*Diagram 56*).

Diagram No. **57**

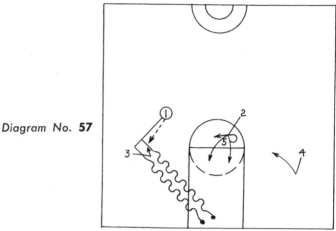

Options off the high post. *Diagram 57* (*above*) illustrates a guard-forward option that can be worked from the same formation. No. 1 has passed to 3 and breaks off hard, using a change-of-pace move to shake his guard and receive either the inside or outside hand-off and set up his drive for the hoop. If 1 is not open on this play, or if he receives the pass from 3 but cannot get to the basket, the player in possession looks for 2 breaking off the back of high post man 5. If none of these ventures is successful, the team can move easily to its high post pattern with 4 breaking across court trying to hang his man up on the post.

Diagram No. **58a**

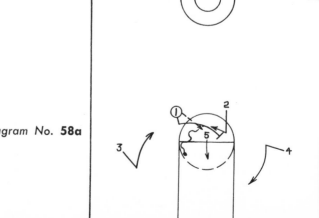

Another option is shown in *Diagram 58a.* The first pass goes to the high post from the guard bringing the ball up. The guard breaks off the post and looks for the hand-off. If he does not receive it, he can stay and set a double screen as 2 breaks off the post or he can continue through and screen for 4 who comes low. If 1 comes off 5 and doesn't hold the double screen, the post-man turns, faces the basket, and looks for 4,

Diagram No. **58b**

breaking off 1's screen (*Diagram 58b*). If the defense switches, 1 has the inside to step in for an easy goal. If 2 comes off a double screen and receives the hand-off from 5, he may have a jump shot inside the circle or perhaps a drive to the basket.

The third option is shown in *Diagram 59.* No. 2 passes to forward 4 who breaks in close to the foul circle. No. 2 breaks off 4 looking for the hand-off. If he does not receive the ball, he sets the double screen with 4 for 1. No. 1 has the jumper or perhaps a drive to the basket.

Diagram 60 (*see next page*) shows another option off the high post attack which resembles the quick opener in football. No. 2 brings the ball up and passes to 3 who breaks toward the ball, often entering the upper foul circle. No. 1 times his move so that he drives off 3 just after he has received the pass from 2. No. 3 hands off to 1 as 1 bursts to the hoop. This move is especially effective against teams which are overplaying the offensive players. If 3 can get good position alongside the foul lane or into the top of the circle, 1 should have little difficulty in cutting hard off 3 and receiving the hand-off. Inasmuch as his defensive man is giving him a step advantage by virtue of his overplaying his postion, 1 can become a real threat.

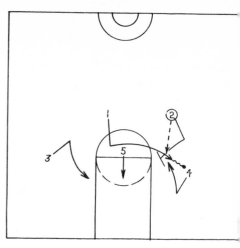

Diagram No. **59**

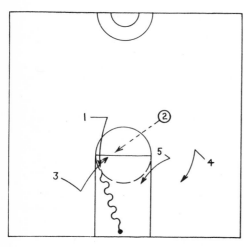

Diagram No. **60**

Diagram No. **61**

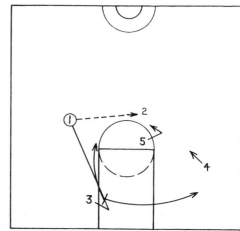

Diagram 61 shows a one-on-one clear-out from the high post formation. In this sequence, No. 3 has taken his position along the foul lane, deep to the basket. No. 1 passes to 2 and moves to screen 3's man. No. 3 takes his man into the screen and breaks out to receive 2's pass in the vicinity of the foul line. No. 3 then turns and faces the basket. Since 1 cleared out after his screen to the opposite side of the court, 3 now has a clear side to work one-on-one with his man. (*Diagram 62, see below.*) This is an excellent play for any situation in which one player is offensively superior to the defensive ability of the individual opponent. We have used this play on one-shot situations at the end of the half or end of the game. We have

Diagram No. **62**

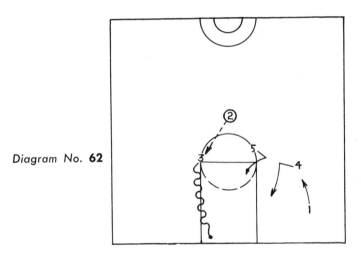

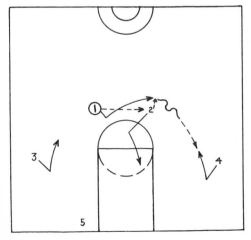

Diagram No. **63**

used this tactic to exploit the defensive weakness of a particular player, or to place a defensive man in personal foul trouble.

LOW POST ATTACK

For situations in which we feel our post-man is superior to the defensive ability of his opponent we may place him in a low post position (*Diagram 63, page 161*). This pattern starts in a way similar to the high post pattern. No. 1 has passed to 2 and receives the return pass. No. 2 moves across to the top of the circle, then as 4 receives 1's pass, 2 changes direction and breaks down the lane. If 2 does not receive the pass from 4, he sets a quick screen for the deep post-man, 5 (*Diagram 64*). No. 5 breaks off the screen toward the ball and is often in position to get his shot immediately with either a hook or a quick stop, turn, and jump shot move.

Diagram No. **64**

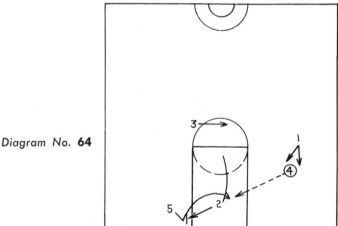

If 5 is not immediately open, 4 hands off to 1 coming off his back and 1 again looks for his drive. No. 4 breaks across and down the lane trying to use 5 as a screen. If 1 has neither the drive nor the pass to 4 cutting down the lane, he feeds the post and executes a split with 3 who comes from the top of the circle (*Diagram 65, see page 163*). If none of these moves produces the good shot, the ball returns to 2 at the top of the circle, and one of the other options or patterns begins.

We have found that by varying our high and low post positions and by utilizing the various options which have been enumerated, we have been

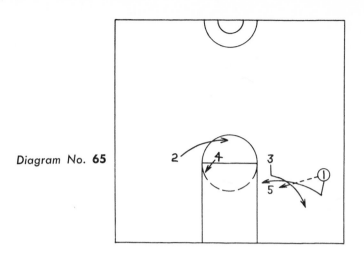

Diagram No. 65

able to obtain a good shot consistently when fast-break opportunities do not materialize.

COACHING TIPS FOR MAN-TO-MAN OFFENSE

1. Use the individual abilities of your players in your team offense.
2. Don't leave the offense to chance—have a definite plan organized for your team.
3. Allow freedom for improvised moves created by defensive change.
4. Drill players until they are thoroughly familiar with the patterns and options you may use.
5. Limit your team offense to basically sound and fundamental plays.
6. Insist on precise execution of the offense.
7. Look for ways to improve your offense.
8. Stress the importance of team play to your players.
9. Stress the value of patience in working for the "good shot."

ZONE OFFENSE

The zone offense should begin from a formation basically the same as that of the man-to-man attack. The similarity of positions facilitates the learning process of the players. *Diagram 66 (see page 164)* shows the 2-3 formation with the high or low post which we have used at St. Joseph's for several seasons. It is a moving offense which combats zone match-up defenses. The play may start from either side with the guard initiating the

play to either the forward on his side or the other guard. He then moves
to the same corner or to the opposite corner.

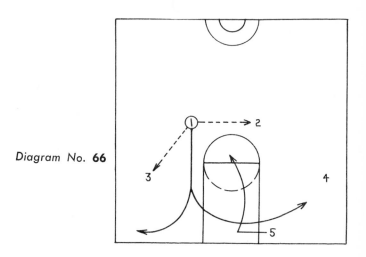

Diagram No. **66**

Diagram 67 shows 1 in the opposite corner. No. 2, who received 1's
pass, has the choice of passing to 5 or 4. In the diagram, he has passed to
4 who passes to 1 on the baseline. No. 4 also has the option of passing to
the high post man 5, who may relay to 3 at the side of the foul lane or, if
the under-basket area is open, 5 passes to 3 cutting into that area.

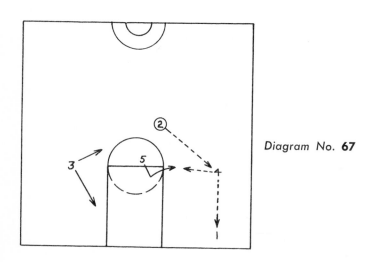

Diagram No. **67**

In *Diagram 68* (*below*), 4 has passed to 1 and either cuts directly to the basket or cuts in back of 5 (similar to the man-to-man move) and then down the lane. No. 1 watches for an open 4. If 4 is not open to receive 1's pass, then 5 breaks down the lane toward the ball. If 1 can hit 5 he does so. No. 5 may have an open lane to the basket, or he may find 4 open on the other side of the foul lane.

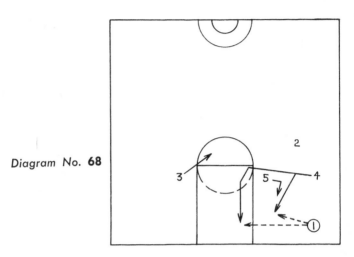

Diagram No. **68**

If 1 cannot pass to 5, he brings the ball out to 2 (*Diagram 69*), who passes to either 3 or 5, as the latter breaks out again to the high post position. No. 3 then hits the side man (4), breaks down the lane off 5's back. Nos. 2 and 1 slide over one position and the offensive continuity is ready to go again (*Diagram 70*).

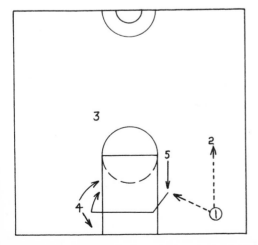

Diagram No. **69**

We find we can work this offense against all zones, whether they are standard formations or attempts at matching up. It is essential that players be aware of all possibilities for scoring and that they take advantage of them with each pass.

Diagram No. 70

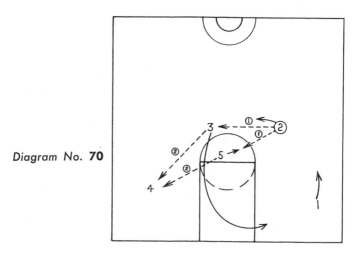

COACHING TIPS FOR ZONE OFFENSE

1. Fast-break the zone defense.
2. Move the ball rapidly with a sharp passing attack.
3. Attempt a quick pass attack to weak side players. Use a post-man as a relay in this tactic.
4. Drive against the zone to draw the defense out and pass under.
5. Drill players on attaining immediate shooting position upon receiving the pass in the zone attack.
6. Rebound viciously against the zone.
7. Beat the defensive player to the area he must cover.
8. Take advantage of all under-the-basket openings.
9. Remember—you must penetrate the zone to beat it.
10. Don't hurry the offense. Work the ball. Move personnel until the good shot is obtained.
11. Capitalize on the fact that zone defensive players are usually poor man-to-man defenders.
12. Draw tough defensive rebounders away from the basket by working the ball into their zone areas.

CHAPTER 12

Situation
Offenses

Attacking the man-to-man press. The method of attacking the full-court man-to-man press depends on the tenacity of the defense. It also depends upon the ball-handling ability of the offensive team. This applies especially to the back-court men. If the offensive back-court is superior to the defense, then it is well to allow the back-court men to advance the ball against their man-to-man opponents and place the remaining players so that the offensive attack may begin as soon as the ball crosses mid-court. This amounts to a clear-out for the better ball-handling guards. The guard advances the ball over mid-court by dribbling, and the offensive attack begins from that point. The second guard maintains a reasonably close position so that if the dribbler is forced to pass or needs a screen, that opportunity is available to him.

If the defense is stronger than the ball-handling ability of the guards, then it becomes imperative to bring a third man into the back-court against the full-court man-to-man press. In *Diagram 71,* front-court man 3 breaks to the foul line position and holds that for screening purposes. Back-court man 2 breaks on either side of 3, using him as a screen to receive the inlet pass from 1. No. 2 is then able to pass to 3 and cut off or use 3 as a screen to advance the ball on the dribble. Back-court man 1 hovers nearby to assist in the advance of the ball. If 4 or 5 is needed, he breaks toward the ball—again acting as a post so that the dribbler may pass and cut to receive a return pass. If the offensive team gains an advantage (two-on-one, three-on-one, or three-on-two), it is exploited to bring about a scoring situation. No. 3, who assisted in this play, is the best ball-handler of

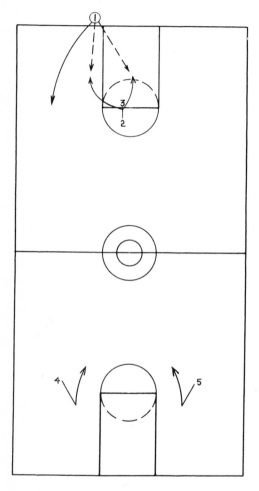

Diagram No. 71

the three front-court men. He is able to obtain post position, hand off well, and dribble so that the ball may be advanced into the front-court.

When man-to-man pressure is applied at half-court, the offensive team must be able to initiate its offense from the half-court position. The multiple man-to-man offense described in the preceding chapter provides numerous scoring opportunities against half-court pressure. By using the high post-

Diagram No. 72

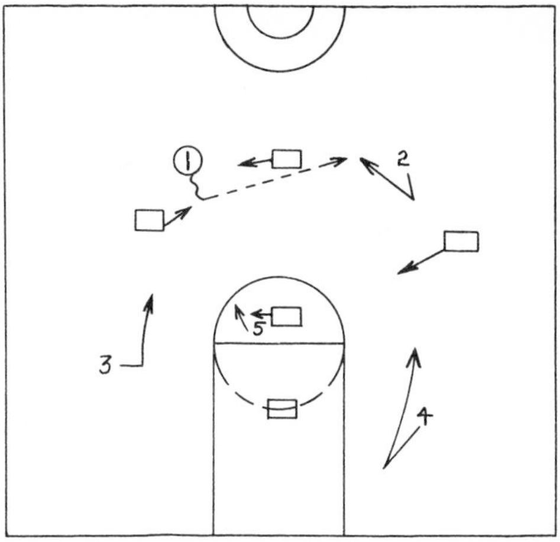

man as illustrated in *Diagram 57 (page 158)*, the back-court men are positioned to obtain easy field goals against the overzealous defense. *Diagram 60, page 160,* illustrates another tactic of merit against the half-court press. Quick openers like these should be a part of the team's planned offense so that half-court pressure can be handled in stride.

Attacking the zone press. *Diagram 72 (see above)* shows a strong attack against the 3-1-1 half-court press. No. 1 has dribbled the ball up to, but not into, the front line pocket. Before becoming enmeshed in the double-up, 1 passes quickly to 2. As the defensive wingman on 2's side of the court advances to begin another double-up, 2 passes to 4, 5 breaks toward the ball, and 1 slides down the opposite side-court along the foul lane (*Diagram 73*). With the ball in the high post position, and

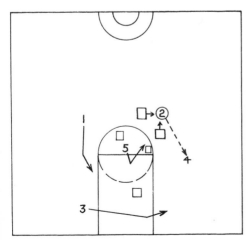

Diagram No. 73

the offense commanding a three-on-one or perhaps a three-on-two advantage, the high post man, 5, is in the position to pass either to 1 or 4 for the short shot (*Diagram 74, below*). If 3 cannot get the ball to 5, he should find 4 open on the baseline from which point 4 has his choice of cutters to the basket—1, 5, or 3. If this sequence does not result in a

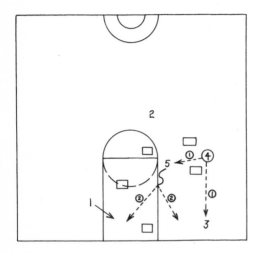

Diagram No. 74

good shot, the ball can be brought out to the front-court and moved to the opposite side where a similar attack begins.

COACHING TIPS ON ATTACKING
THE PRESSING DEFENSE

Man-to-man press

1. Clear out for the skilled ball-handler so that he may advance the ball into the front-court position.
2. Include within your offensive framework opportunities to move quickly into a *planned* offense as the ball crosses mid-court.
3. Avoid lateral movements involving the ball by which the defense is drawn into favorable double-up positions.
4. Always move directly toward the ball when receiving a pass.
5. If the defensive man is overplaying so well that his man cannot get the ball, the offensive man must screen for a teammate so that the latter is in position to receive a pass.

6. Use "back-door" maneuvers to free cutters against the man-to-man press.
7. Use the post for outlet passing and cutting opportunities.
8. Practice situations in which the defense applies pressure to the offensive team.
9. Make certain that your team *attacks* the press.

Zone press

1. Use a minimum of dribbling.
2. Come to meet all passes.
3. Get rid of the ball before a double-up takes place.
4. Penetrate the zone press with a sharp passing attack aimed at its weakest points.
5. Break cutters into open scoring areas near the basket.
6. The objective is to *score*—not to hold the ball.
7. Your team will have confidence in a well-organized, thoroughly practiced attack.

The "stall" situation. There often comes a time in a ball game when a coach wants his team to work a little more carefully for a good shot. Such situations may exist with his team holding a six-point lead with four minutes to go. This is too long a period for an all-out freeze, and yet the coach will want his team to be just a bit more conservative with its shots. If the opponent is playing a zone defense, the coach may want to draw the opponent out of the zone by maintaining possession beyond the foul circle.

If the opponent is playing man-to-man defense, in the same situation, the offensive team may do well to stay within its pattern until the high percentage shot (inside the foul line) is obtained. The offensive team *does not* want to stop its attack. It must threaten to score during this stall, and occasionally, the offensive team will do well to burst through on a quick offensive play. Such maneuvers will often catch the defensive team off balance and provide further insurance for the team in the lead. The objective of the stall offense is to maintain or increase the team's lead—not merely to maintain possession of the ball.

FREEZE OFFENSE

The freeze situation arises when the leading team is protecting an advantage so narrow that it dares not give up the ball unless the defense allows an unmolested lay-up shot or fouls a player on the offensive team in its efforts to obtain possession of the ball. A team in such a situation must consistently threaten to score. It must position its players so that they will be able to take advantage of defensive lapses.

Man-to-man freeze. In a situation as described above, in which the defensive team is employing a man-to-man defense, the offensive team may do well to freeze by allowing its best ball-handler to carry out a one-man freeze. We have been fortunate in recent years to have the services of an outstanding dribbler. This player has enabled us to win many close games by maintaining possession of the ball for extended periods of time. The dribbling skill of this player coupled with his high percentage foul shooting proved to be a very happy combination for us.

In such situations, the other back-court man (or other good ball-handler) stands by to provide outlet relief in the event that the dribbler becomes tied up or is doubled-up. The other players stay out of the way.

Another important position in the one-man freeze is the post-man. The post-man must constantly be aware of his responsibility to serve as a receiver of an outlet pass should the dribbler require it. If the post-man handles the ball, he should return it to the dribbler as quickly as is safely possible, then clear away until he is needed again.

Moving freeze pattern. The team without the skilled dribbler must resort to a moving offense in order to maintain possession and to threaten

Diagram No. **75**

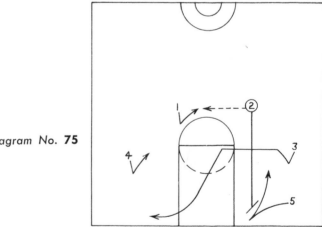

to score. For several seasons, when St. Joseph's lacked the exceptional ball-handler, we utilized a five-man moving attack against man-to-man pressure. We were very gratified with the results of this move. The offensive formation we used is described in *Diagram 75*.

Nos. 1 and 2 are the back-court men; 3 and 4 take side positions, and 5 plays the deep post moved out toward the corner. The play may start from either side. In the diagram, 2 has possession and passes to 1. He screens inside for 3 who takes his man in and then cuts off the screen. If this player has succeeded in hanging his man on the screen and the lane is open for his drive, 1 passes him the ball and 3 goes in for the lay-up.

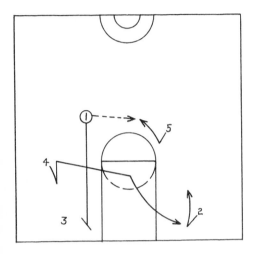

Diagram No. **76**

Most frequently, however, 3 is not open on this play. His maneuver does serve to keep the defense honest, however, and also opens up the passing lane so that 5, coming off the screen that 2 sets for him near the baseline, breaks out toward the ball and receives the pass from 1 (*Diagram 76*). After passing to 5, 1 screens inside as 4 cuts through the lane to the opposite baseline. No. 1 continues and screens 3's man as 3 breaks out to receive 5's pass. This movement continues with the offensive team constantly threatening to score by taking advantage of any defensive lapse.

Any player who is overplayed so that he cannot receive a pass, screens back inside so that he is replaced by the next man on his way out. This freeze pattern serves not only as an effective end-of-game technique but also may be used as a stall offense. Occasionally we have even used this formation as our basic offense and have found that it provided us with a good number of jump shots and drives through the lane.

This pattern can be used to excellent advantage as a stall offense. The continuity of movement and the constant threat of the scoring play make this pattern functional for "hold until the lay-up" situations.

ZONE FREEZE

If the pressing team is using a zone defense, the freezing team should use its attack for the zone press. The only difference in the two attacks is that the offensive team will limit its shooting to the short lay-up shot. The freezing team may also want to "string out" the zone press so that (refer to *Diagram 72*) the offensive players use the whole court area and will make longer passes. In such situations the freezing team can utilize a 2-1-2 attack and throw to the four corners of the half-court and use the post-man as an outlet in the event of an emergency. Here again, however, the freezing team must threaten to score. If they do not, the pressing defensive team will feel safe in taking as many chances as possible— knowing the offensive team is not going to shoot anyway.

COACHING TIPS ON THE FREEZE OFFENSE

1. Threaten to score.
2. Take only the unmolested lay-up shot.
3. Come to meet all passes.
4. Make certain your team has its best foul shooters in the game during the freeze situation.
5. Whenever possible, leave the ball-handling to the most skilled on the squad.
6. Don't go into the freeze too early in a ball game. It can cause your team to lose its offensive momentum and provide the pressing team with just the opportunity it needs to get back in the ball game.
7. Work on freeze situations frequently at practice. Use the timer and referees to assure game-like conditions.
8. Confront the players with end-of-game foul shooting situations at practice; *e.g.*: "You have one and one to shoot, you're one point ahead and there are seven seconds to play."
9. Avoid double-team situations.
10. Save at least two times-out for use at the end of the game.

CHAPTER 13

Special Considerations

How many times has a coach said to himself at a crucial point of the ball game, "We have just got to get possession of this jump ball"? How many times has your opponent scored easy field goals against your team with simple out-of-bounds maneuvers?

These two aspects of the game are too important to overlook. A good team has set maneuvers on both jump ball and out-of-bounds situations to assure the attainment of definite objectives. Proper organization of these two factors by the coach and a few minutes of practice each session will pay big dividends to the team.

THE JUMP BALL SITUATION

In college basketball we expect an average of seven jump ball situations per game, including the tap plays at the opening of the game and at the beginning of the second half. High school competition will provide more opportunities for this particular situation. We feel that if we get possession of the ball each time there is a jump ball situation, we have taken a big step toward winning the game. This means we have seven more scoring opportunities than our opponent. We strive to obtain a high percentage of possessions from the situation. To do this we have definite formations—one which we apply at mid-court and at the defensive foul circle; a second which we employ at the offensive foul circle.

Use of signals. Clear, easily understood signals are given by the player involved in the jump ball situation to indicate the direction of his tap if he feels he can control it, or to indicate he will assist the opponent in tapping to the defensive front-court. These signals may take the form of hand or arm motions, foot signals, touching on the skin or the uniform, or any other set of symbols that will be easily recognized by all members of the team.

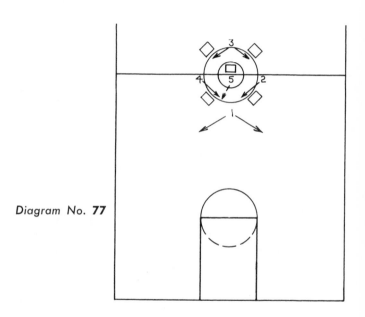

Diagram No. **77**

Jump ball formations. The formation shown in *Diagram 77* is that used by St. Joseph's on jump balls at mid-court. On this particular tap, No. 5 signals for a defensive tap. He has indicated to his teammates his doubts about controlling the tap, therefore, he will assist his opponent in tapping the ball to the defensive front-court. Nos. 4 and 2 break through and crash hard and high in front of the opponent's front-court men. If either can get a hand on the ball, he taps it over the head of the opponent to a position deeper in the back-court where 1 will retrieve the ball. Since most teams like to tap up front, we have been able to obtain a good percentage of possessions through this technique even though our opponent has a height advantage in the actual jump ball situation and controls the direction of the tap. If the opponent's jumper back-taps, 3 is ready to cut in front of either man in his efforts to steal the ball.

If, at the mid-court jump ball, 5 feels confident that he is able to control the tap, he may tap up front to 3 or he may tap deep into the

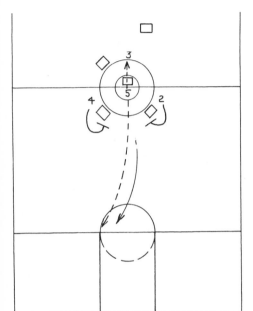

Diagram No. **78**

back-court to 1, who takes advantage of 4's block on the opponent's front-court man to obtain possession. (*Diagram 78*).

If our opponent lines up in a formation similar to our own, then we position our players as shown in *Diagram 79*. If 5 feels he can control the tap, he will signal the direction of his tap. If 3 is in a good position at the top of the circle, 5 will tap to him. If there is some possibility of the defensive cut-off, 5 will tap back to whichever side he has indicated by signal. The diagram shows the tap back deep to the left back-court position. No. 1 checks his man off and 4, getting a jump with the tap, hustles into the back-court to retrieve the ball. Any time the ball is tapped to the front-court, the two wingmen (4 and 2) are in good position to break and create a three-on-one or a three-on-two situation. They must wait, however, to be certain that 3 has obtained possession of the ball. Those occasions where 3 relays 5's tap with one of his own to the breaking wingmen are very limited, and actually present a hazardous attempt to score.

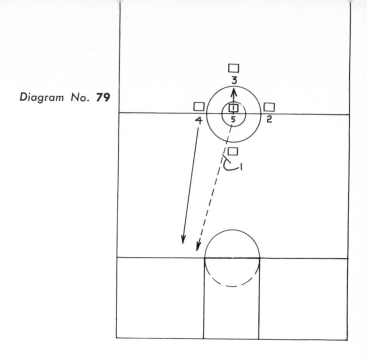

Diagram No. **79**

For jump ball situations at the offensive foul circle we line up two and two (*Diagram 80*). In this diagram, No. 3 indicates the direction of his tap if he feels he can get control. If the opponent is two-and-two also and 3 controls the tap, he should be able to place the ball so that 4 or 5 will get possession. If 3 feels uncertain about controlling the tap, he will indicate a defensive formation whereby 4 and 5 will edge up slightly and break through in front of the front men. Teams are reluctant to tap back at their defensive foul line so that either 4 or 5 has a reasonably good chance of getting a hand on the ball to tap back to 1 or 2 for possession.

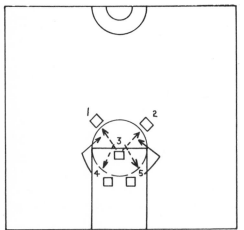

Diagram No. **80**

Diagram 81 (*see below*) shows the formation at the defensive end of the court on held-ball situations. Once more we return to our mid-court formation. Numbers 4 and 3 move closer to the offensive front-court men, and 5 plays between them. No. 5 is responsible for recovering long taps

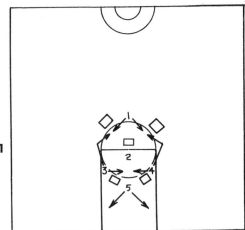

Diagram No. **81**

in either direction toward the basket. Numbers 3 and 4 are responsible for knifing in front of the opponent and getting possession of the ball. If it appears that the opponent will back-tap, 3 or 4 has the option of cutting in front of the deep player in an effort to tap the ball to 1. This occurs only if the opponent has tipped his hand *openly* as to the tap play. Ordinarily, 1 will knife in front of either of the back men if the ball is tapped backwards by the opponent.

COACHING TIPS ON JUMP BALL SITUATIONS

1. Work out an easily understood set of signals for proper positioning and movements on jump ball situations.
2. Practice jump ball situations frequently.
3. Provide practice in tapping the tossed ball for each player— not just the big boys on your squad.
4. Never concede the opponent possession of the tap even though he may control it.
5. Use your "leapers" for cut-off men on jump balls. Use the smallest man in a safety position except at the defensive foul circle.

6. Use the biggest man among the non-jumpers as the front tap receiver.

Out-of-bounds plays. The use of definite set plays when your team has possession of the ball in the front court provides a good opportunity to score. While these opportunities are best when the ball is out-of-bounds on the baseline, they can also be exploited with the ball at side-court position. Out-of-bounds plays should be simple movements which will free a player for a good quick shot. Therefore, the plays should be uncomplicated. Following are some plays which we have used or had used against us. They should give the coach an idea of the effectiveness of the simple play.

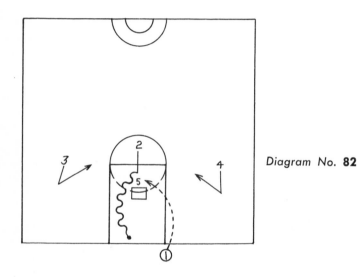

Diagram No. **82**

Diagram 82 shows a formation with a ball out-of-bounds on the baseline. The team's big man, No. 5, takes his position just in back of the dotted line in the foul lane (remember he may stay in there as long as he wants until the ball is inbounds and has touched someone). No. 1, taking the ball out of bounds, delivers a high pass to 5 if he is being faceguarded by his opponent. No. 5 leaps high, catches the ball and shoots while in the air. This is an especially good play for a 6'4" or a 6'5" leaper who can get up over his defender.

If 5 does not have a good shot after receiving the pass, he may then turn and hand off as 2 drives down the lane. Numbers 3 and 4 "juke" their men in and out to keep them occupied.

A second option from this play occurs when 5, faking his anticipation of the pass from out-of-bounds, takes a step backward and, still facing the basket, holds his position while 2 runs his man into 5's back and breaks to either side to receive 1's pass. Again, numbers 3 and 4 keep their opponents occupied (*Diagram 83*).

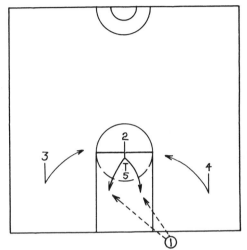

Diagram No. 83

Another formation for out-of-bounds play is shown in *Diagram 84*. On signal (usually a slap of the ball), 2 breaks to the opposite side of the lane and screens 5's man (turning to the basket as he does so). No. 5 runs his man into 2 and breaks across the lane. If 2 has set an effective screen and there is no switch, 5 will be open to receive 1's pass for the lay-up shot. If there is a switch, 2 can step in and receive 1's pass with his man on his back.

Diagram No. 84

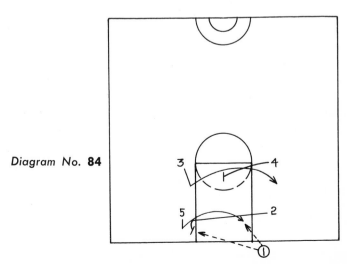

No. 4 moves into the lane about a step later than 2's screen and screens for 3 who runs his man off. This may result in a short jumper for 3 if neither 2 nor 5 is open on the initial play. At least it will provide 1 with a passing outlet if the intended play does not materialize.

Another option from this formation is shown in *Diagram 85 (see below)*. In this play 5 moves two steps backward to set a block for 3, who runs his man off to the outside. Again, if an effective screen is set and there is no switch, 3 will be open for the lay-up. If there is a switch, 5 will be

Diagram No. **85**

able to break toward the basket to receive 1's pass with the defender on his back. After waiting a second, No. 4 takes his man in and uses 2 as a screen to free himself for the jumper if neither 3 nor 5 is open. As in the first option, 4 can be counted on as the outlet if the original play does not work.

Many teams forego any out-of-bounds formations when the opponent lines up in a zone defense. The zone is also susceptible to out-of-bounds plays. *Diagram 86 (see page 183)* shows a simple but effective formation with the ball out-of-bounds on the baseline. Most teams using a zone defense will fall into a 2-3 or a 2-1-2 defense with the ball out-of-bounds on the baseline. In this particular play, 5 stands in the lane to occupy the middle defensive man. Numbers 2 and 4 take positions toward the sideline to occupy the defensive men in those areas. No. 3 starts from the foul line, breaks through to either side of the defensive man occupied by 5. If the defensive man moves to cover 3, then 5 is open; if he stays with 5, then 3 is open for the short jump shot.

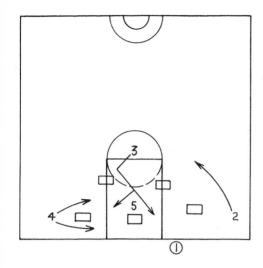

Diagram No. **86**

With the ball out-of-bounds on the side-court, the team in possession frequently is able to break a quick play from its offensive sequence. *Diagram 87* illustrates such a play from the framework of our high post man-to-man offense. No. 1 passes the ball from out of bounds to 4, who breaks in and out to meet the pass. As the pass is made to 4, 2 rubs his man off the back of the high post (5). No. 4 turns and looks for 2 cutting. If he does not find 2 open, he has another potential pass receiver in 3 who also uses 5 as a screen and breaks across the foul line. A quick move like this will often catch the defensive team off guard momentarily and allow a quick field goal.

Diagram No. **87**

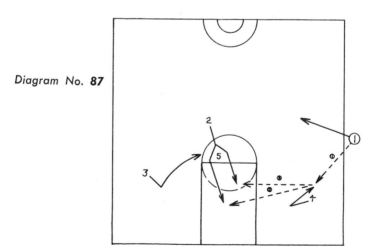

This play may be used from mid-court as well. It is an excellent maneuver to use in a situation in which your team is one or two points behind or tied with seconds remaining and you need that quick score.

COACHING TIPS ON OUT-OF-BOUNDS PLAYS

Offense

1. Use basically sound and fundamental moves in out-of-bounds plays.
2. Keep plays as simple as possible.
3. Devise a set of easily understood signals to classify each play.
4. Utilize the individual offensive ability of the players.
5. Use the same formation for a variety of out-of-bounds plays.
6. Flood the close-to-the-basket areas against the zone defense.
7. Always have a safety valve outlet in the event that the expected play does not materialize.
8. Have a good passer take the ball out-of-bounds.

Defense

1. Never permit the opponent to obtain the short shot from the out-of-bounds position. Sag off to force the opponent to pass the ball deep into the back-court.
2. Fight through all the screens rather than switch.
3. The defender playing the man out-of-bounds must force the pass-in away from the basket area and then clog the lanes against any cutter after the pass-in is made.

PART 3

The Season

CHAPTER 14

Training
the Team

Cutting the squad. One of the most difficult tasks which confronts the coach each year is that of cutting the squad. Although this is an unpleasant job, it must be done. It is impossible to work effectively with a large number of players. I am convinced that the *best* squad is a *small* one. I like to carry 10 players on the team. With this number each member becomes a playing part of the team. The coach is able to work intensely with each player at practice and is usually able to find a need for each in the game.

Once the coach decides on the number of players he wants on the squad, he should bring his team to that number as soon as he feels he has seen enough of the players to know their ability. The longer a player hangs on, the more difficult it becomes to cut him.

In selecting his squad the coach must consider his needs at the various positions. It would be foolish to carry six back-court men, when the coach knows he won't use more than three or four during the season. It would seem equally shortsighted to carry a squad of big men without anyone to handle the ball. The coach's needs depend upon the kind of game he plays on offense and defense, his policy of substituting, and the material among the teams he will be facing during the season. For example, a coach might be inclined to retain a big boy who is not well developed so that he would have someone to play against an opponent's known big man.

Large squads often become spawning grounds for discontent. As the season progresses, the last players on the squad of 15 often become more and more dissatisfied with their bench-sitting role. They begin to see themselves as possessing more ability than they actually have. Such morale problems can be avoided by limiting the number of squad members to those who will play.

Conditioning players. Many coaches advocate cross-country running, jogging on the track, wind sprints, calesthenics, and other similar activities to increase the stamina of their players. While this will undoubtedly accomplish that objective, I feel that there are other more practical methods of bringing the basketball player up to playing condition.

The coach who is limited in the length of his preseason practice may, of necessity, have to rely on these procedures so that his squad is physically prepared to enter strenuously into the opening day's activities. If that is the situation, the coach will find that a week's outdoor running will be of great benefit. The running program should start with a mile jog on the first day, and build up to two one-mile distance runs by the end of the week. Wind sprints (in which the runner does not quite go all out) are introduced on the second day and continued through the week. These are of the run (25 yards) and jog (25 yards) description. A half-mile of such sprints and jogs each day will develop the stamina of the player. By the end of the week, the players are jogging a mile, wind sprinting a half-mile, then jogging a final mile.

I like to combine conditioning exercises with practice in the skills demanded by the defensive and offensive aspects of the game. Therefore, our players attain playing condition by running in ball-handling, shooting, and defensive drills. We have them work full-court one-on-one drills. They run in our fast-break drills. All of these activities accomplish our basketball objectives while conditioning the players at the same time.

The conditioning of basketball players has never seemed a great problem to me. I feel that after a month's practice, our squad is in physical condition to play the season. Once the squad reaches this point, the coach must be careful to maintain it. He should resist the urge to over-practice or over-condition the players when things are not going as well as he would like.

Over-conditioning is manifest in the symptoms called staleness. Staleness is most often an emotional characteristic. It becomes evident when a player or players become "tired of playing." Stale players become listless, inattentive, and lose their playing edge. This is the time when the coach should give a player, or perhaps the whole squad, a day off from practice and suggest a change in routine. This situation may occur during the preseason practice session, as well as in the latter stages of the game season.

The coach must be on the lookout for symptoms of staleness and take steps to alleviate this condition.

Isotonic and isometric exercise programs. In recent years basketball coaches have been using weight training programs to increase the over-all strength and jumping ability of their players. This movement began in the early 1950's in apparent contradiction to the theory that basketball players had to be built on the "lean side" if they were to achieve success. Weight lifting of any kind had been frowned upon.

The initial experiments in this kind of activity were primarily leg exercises in which the individuals performed "squats" and "toe risers" while supporting enough weight across the shoulders to limit the repetition of such exercises to ten. These and other exercises were tested successfully upon basketball players at the college level by the late Bucky O'Connor, basketball coach at the University of Iowa. Coach O'Connor reported that his players experienced an average increase in their vertical jumping ability of slightly better than two inches with a maximum individual increase of seven inches. These exercises were "isotonic," which means the tension in the muscles remains unchanged and that there is a shortening of the muscles used during the performance of the exercise. The most common form of the isotonic exercise is weight lifting.

More recently, the practice of "isometric" contraction has become very popular. Theoretically, this means that, during the contraction of the muscle, the *length* of the muscle involved in the exercise remains unchanged. (Muscles engaged in *isometric* contraction actually shorten slightly, while muscles in *isotonic* contraction shorten appreciably during the performance of the exercise.) The most common technique of the isometric exercise is the exertion of force against an immovable object from various positions so that different muscle groups are used. Experimenters in the isometric form of exercise have come up with two especially pertinent findings: (1) They have found that increase in muscle strength can be developed at its maximum rate by exerting from 40 to 60 percent of potential strength in a *single* isometric contraction of *a few seconds duration once a day* during an eight-week period. (2) The newly acquired strength can be maintained with a minimum amount of further isometric training. (Experiments have indicated that such a level can be maintained by exercising once every two weeks for an additional eight-week period.)

Actually the difference between isometric and isotonic contractions is slight. Isotonic exercises (weight lifting, for example) become isometric when the point of greatest effort is reached. However, the practice of isometric contractions appears to be more easily accomplished. The important point for coaches to consider is that muscle development can be increased at a rapid rate by brief periods of overwork. This has easy application to all sports—but especially to basketball.

These findings startled and interested scores of coaches and athletes. The theory presented a new and more practical approach to weight training for athletes.

1. Since the isometric exercises were of brief duration, it was no longer necessary for athletes to work extensively to obtain the gains in strength achieved by a repetition of isotonic exercises.
2. The gains experienced seemed to be greater than those obtained from isotonic exercises.
3. Since fatigue was not a factor in isometric exercise, it seemed plausible that athletes might work out with the isometric regimen while their sport was in season.
4. Once the athlete gained in strength, it would be possible for him to maintain that increment with only brief application of these exercises in the future.

The basketball coach is certainly interested in the improvement of over-all strength of his players and, especially, as this added strength effects the increase in their ability to jump. I wanted to find out if isometric contraction exercises could do this for my players. I had read that Bob Pettit, the great St. Louis *Hawks* player, had completed a training course in isometric exercise and had found that it had aided him in his jumping and in providing added strength. However, before I set up a program for the players on my squad, I wanted to try it myself and discover what it could do for me—at 36 years of age! I obtained from Bob Hoffman, of the York Barbell Company (York, Pa.), a set of eight exercises. I performed them daily. At the end of each week I tested my jumping ability. Each week there was some increase until, at the end of the sixth week, I was jumping *seven* inches higher than when I began! That was enough for me. I was sold on the idea! My players, who had watched the progress of the exercise program (with amused interest, initially) shared my enthusiasm.

I proceeded to work up a less extensive program, eliminating those exercises which did not seem to be of benefit to the basketball player and adjusting the technique of performance as I read more about the theories and practices of isometric contraction. The program, described in the succeeding pages, is what I settled upon as most beneficial to the player for accomplishing the objectives of added over-all strength and increased vertical jumping ability. There are five exercises in the routine to be performed daily. The recommended length of the program is eight weeks, then one day every two weeks for eight more weeks. Participants must loosen up with a brief period of calisthenics before beginning the exercises. They then proceed to complete the five exercises—pausing long enough to adjust the exercise bar to the desired level. Each player can accomplish the program in about 10 minutes—and that includes the time taken for the calisthenics.

In working with my basketball squad, I have found universal benefit and approval. Also:

1. Jumping distance improved an average of two inches.
2. Players reported "feeling stronger."
3. Players acquired the ability to jump easier and shoot with greater facility. (This was especially true of the jump shot.)

One of our 5'8" back-court men, after a week's work with isometrics, jumped up and grabbed the rim for the first time in his life. One lanky 6'8" lad went from 195 pounds to 215—all muscle—during the summer months.

Except for one player, whose chronic knee injury seemed to be aggravated by the exercises, the evidence has been decidedly positive. I feel isometric contraction has great value in the conditioning of basketball players. I also utilized the overload theory in drilling on offensive fundamentals. I found that skills in passing, dribbling, and shooting can be increased by using a ball heavier than the basketball—a medicine ball or "heavyweight basketball," for example. During the past season, we spent a portion of each day of preseason practice working on passing skills, using these implements for brief daily periods. The improvement of the players in these skills was immediately noticeable. They passed more accurately and for greater distance. There was more "snap" to their passes. After working with the heavyweight ball, their dribbling was better controlled and their shooting became an effortless task. The shooting accuracy of the players increased because they no longer had to "strain" with a shot. Players were able to shoot the jumper from the fringe of the circle with greater ease and accuracy. Weighted shoes and vests have also proved effective for the development of the strength of the player. By increasing the work that the muscles must do, increase in strength will result. Improvement in performance will generally follow.

*   *   *

Coaches who want to read more intensively on the theories of this technique might consult the works of Arthur H. Steinhaus, of George

William College, Chicago, Ill. Dr. Steinhaus has written extensively on the development of strength. An article germane to isometric theory and practice is *Training for Strength: Isometric Contraction,* Croft Educational Services, New London, Conn.

Other works of interest on this subject include: *Physiology of Exercises,* by Laurence E. Morehouse and Augustine T. Miller, C. V. Mosby Co., St. Louis, 1953; *Psychology of Coaching,* by John D. Lawther, Prentice-Hall, Inc., Englewood Cliffs, N. J., 1955; *Physiology of Muscular Activity,* by Peter V. Karpovich, W. B. Saunders, Philadelphia, 1959.

ISOMETRIC EXERCISES

Exercise 1 Place the exercise bar in a position at which the exerciser does not fully extend the arms overhead when he grasps it. Face the bar and grip it firmly with the hands, shoulder width apart. With feet flat on the floor, tighten leg, buttock, stomach, and back muscles, exhale, and push against the bar firmly (40-60 percent maximum) for 6 seconds. (*Figure 33a*)

Exercise 2 Place the bar in a position slightly above shoulder level. Stand in front of the bar so that it rests on the shoulders and the back of the neck. Grasp the bar with the hands, shoulder width apart. Tighten leg, buttock, stomach, and back muscles, exhale, and rise on toes, pushing 40-60 percent maximum on the bar with the shoulders and back of the neck for 6 seconds. (*Figure 33b*)

Exercise 3 Place the bar at chin level. Face the bar and grip it firmly with the hands, shoulder width apart. With the feet flat on the floor, tighten leg, buttock, stomach, and back muscles, exhale, and push against the bar 40-60 percent maximum effort for 6 seconds. (*Figure 33c*)

Exercise 4 Place the bar a few inches below waist level. Face the bar and grip it firmly with the hands, shoulder width apart. With feet flat on the floor, tighten leg, back, buttock, and stomach muscles, exhale and pull up (40-60 percent maximum effort) for 6 seconds, while rising on toes. (*Figure 33d*)

Exercise 5 Place the bar a few inches below shoulder level. Stand in front of the bar so that it rests on the shoulders and back of the neck. Grip the bar firmly with the hands, shoulder width apart. Keep the back straight and feet flat on the floor, exhale, and push against the bar 40-60 percent maximum effort for 6 seconds. (*Figure 33e*)

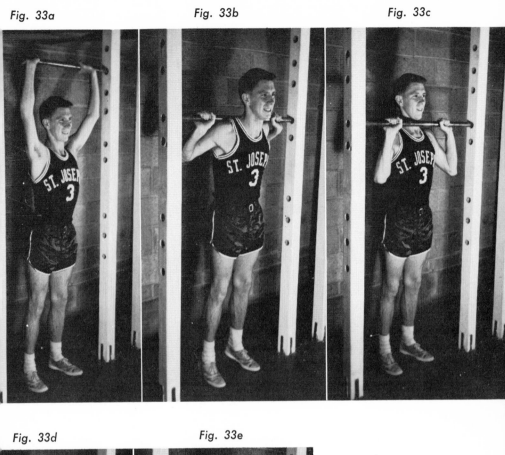

Fig. 33, a-e:
Isometric Exercises

Isometric Equipment. Barbell companies have complete isometric exercise racks ready for distribution. These are excellent. For some budgets, however, the cost of this equipment is prohibitive. The equipment pictured in the accompanying figures is homemade. It was assembled by securing a pair of 4 by 4's to floor and ceiling, then drilling a series of holes on the inside faces at three-inch intervals. The posts are secured so that there is a 36-inch interval between them. A steel bar is used as the exercise piece. The bar is easily adjusted for the varying demands of the different sized players. If two exercise units are constructed, the holes in one unit can be drilled at an interval alternate to that of the other.

Injuries. Injuries are likely to occur during the course of a basketball season. They are like the big men of your opponents—it seems that you're bound to face them every year. If the team has a trainer, it is his duty to care for the minor mishaps and minister to the general welfare of the players. This involves treating a long list of maladies including jammed fingers, skin abrasions, minor cuts and bruises, ingrown toenails, sprains, shin splints, blisters, calluses, charleyhorses, and pre-game jitters. The trainer reports to the coach the occurrence of any injury as well as the steps he has taken to assist the player. He should be on hand at least one hour in advance of the starting time for practice and games to care for the above and to perform whatever taping, wrapping, and diathermy treatment is needed. The trainer should have at his disposal a well-stocked medicine kit. (The efficient trainer is a great asset to the team and a godsend to the coach.)

In many high school situations, however, a trainer is not available. The coach's job thus becomes compounded by this additional duty. He must acquire the skills necessary to perform this job well. Red Cross courses in first aid are helpful to attain this objective.

(*The Athletic Trainer's Handbook,* by Rollie Bevans, Prentice-Hall, Inc., Englewood Cliffs, N. J., 1955, and *Helpful Hints From the First-Aider,* by the Cramer Chemical Co., Gardner, Kansas, will prove beneficial to both the coach or trainer.)

Whether the coach or trainer cares for the minor injuries of the squad, neither should attempt to handle injuries which are potentially serious. Such injuries are to be referred to competent medical authorities. It is an excellent practice to have a doctor in attendance at all games. There is usually at least one doctor in the community willing to take on this responsibility.

Ankle injuries warrant special consideration in any book on basketball. Because of the high incidence of ankle sprains in basketball, the coach will do well to take any precautionary measures he deems necessary to prevent the occurrence of this injury. At St. Joseph's, we require all players with a history of ankle injury—no matter how slight—to be taped for each practice and game. Since most players are unable to avoid this injury at some point in their basketball careers, most of our players are taped for each practice and game. If tape is not available due to budget limitations, ankle wraps will suffice.

The coach must remember that any injury at practice can be just as disastrous as one which occurs during the game. Preparation for practice requires the same careful attention that is given for the games.

Diet. Basketball players expend a tremendous amount of energy in the daily rigors of practice and game competition. This hectic pace demands that the participants adhere to a nutritious diet. I have found most players possess good appetites. Unless a player departs radically from the generally accepted conception of a balanced diet, I feel he will satisfy his own nutritional needs. We do recommend, however, the addition of multi-vitamin pills and wheat germ to the diet during the season.

Some players need guidance in their choice of food. For these players we recommend the selection of foods from among the following:

Breakfast:

        Fresh fruit or fruit juice
        Hot or cold cereal
        Eggs
        Ham or bacon
        Toast and beverage

Avoid: fried foods and doughy products (hot cakes, waffles, pastry).

Lunch:

        Lean meat and fresh vegetable platters
        Meat sandwiches on whole wheat or rye bread
        Salad sandwiches on whole wheat or rye bread
        Beverage
        Light dessert (ice cream, jello, pudding, or candy bar).

Avoid: too much white bread, fried foods and heavy desserts (cake, pie, sundaes, etc.)

Dinner:

        Fruit, fruit juice or salad
        Lean meat (preferably beef)
        Green vegetable
        Potato (baked, broiled, or boiled)
        Beverage
        Light dessert.

Avoid: fatty meats, gravy, and heavy desserts.

The active basketball player seems to snack almost incessantly. I find no quarrel with this practice as long as it does not interfere with the appetite for the main meal. Players should drink plenty of liquids—water, milk or tea. Coffee may be taken in moderate amounts. (We often supply Cokes at half-time for our players to sip. We open the bottles *well in advance of the half* so that the fizz is reduced. The ample supply of sugar in this beverage helps to restore the player's energy.)

Rest. Besides playing basketball and eating, I find that sleep is tops on most players' lists of favorite occupations. The active player requires eight to ten hours of sleep in order to be properly rested. This is very often difficult to attain because of study requirements and practice and game commitments. The coach should encourage the players to nap—even short naps are valuable—when the opportunity presents itself. Each player must work out a system for himself to allow adequate rest, study, and practice time.

Smoking and drinking. The coach cannot condone smoking and drinking. Both of these practices have been found to be of unquestionable harm to the individual. The coach who expects maximum performance from each of his players cannot accept a smoker or a drinker on his team. This is a difficult area for the coach to supervise. Practically speaking, he cannot. If a player wants to indulge, he will find the time and place to do so without the coach's knowledge.

The coach must appeal, therefore, to the integrity of the player. He must point out that the team needs the best performance it can get from each player in order to succeed. The only way each player can give his best performance is through the adoption of good training habits. The vast majority of players will respond to such an appeal. Players should be made to realize the selfishness of any undesirable practice. If the coach discovers that a player has been breaking training, he must take disciplinary action. In most instances a player who smokes or drinks does not have the best interests of the team at heart. The team is well rid of this player. Whatever disciplinary action the coach stipulates for the offense of breaking training, he must inform the squad of the punishment for such infractions *before* the season begins. If there are violations of these regulations, disciplinary action must be meted out without exception.

CHAPTER 15

Game

Preparation

Once the pre-season training is completed and the squad is well-conditioned and well-trained in its defensive and offensive maneuvers, the coach must ready his team for individual games. To do this properly, the coach must obtain as much information as possible about his opponents. He obtains this information by scouting his rivals. The coach should scout his opponents personally, when at all possible. The scouting should be done as near to the time of the actual game as possible. (It would be foolhardy to scout an opponent in December when the game with that team is in late February or early March.)

Scouting. What does the coach look for when scouting a future opponent? The first things to watch are the opponent's *team maneuvers.* This includes team defense, team offense, out-of-bounds plays, and jump ball formations.

In checking the opponent's defense, the coach looks for rules of operation. What does the team do consistently in checking the opponent's offense? The coach notes any team weaknesses. Perhaps the team fails to adequately cover some area in its zone. It may be slow getting back on defense against the fast break. It may be susceptible to the give-and-go attack. It may have weak rebounding. The team may be weak picking up men. These are team considerations which the coach must observe.

In considering team offense, the coach charts any patterns or set plays which the opponent attempts to carry out. He notes attempts to clear out a side for the driver, methods of screening, and charts court positions from which shots are taken. Those things which apply to the team offense are of great importance. The most important task in scouting the opponent is to find out what he does as a team—offensively and defensively.

The scout watches out-of-bounds plays so that these may be carefully defended against at every position. He also observes the jump ball situations to see if the opponent follows a consistent tapping pattern. (One of our opponents in recent years tapped to the same man each time from the center position. Knowledge of this factor enabled us to steal four vital taps when we played the team.)

Individual considerations. In checking the individuals, it is imperative to note particular habits which they are certain to have acquired.

Defense

1. Does the man turn his head to follow the ball exclusively?
2. Is he susceptible to a fake and drive?
3. Does he play well off his man, allowing the quick shot?
4. Does he check the rebounder?
5. Is he easily driven on?
6. Is he slow getting back on defense?
7. Does he permit his man good position to receive a pass or rebound?
8. Are his reactions quick or slow?

All of these factors give us a pretty good picture of the defensive ability of the player, whether his team plays man-to-man or zone defense.

Offense

1. Can the player drive both ways?
2. Is he a good jump shooter?
3. What is his range with the jump shot?
4. Does he handle the ball well?
5. Is he a good passer in either direction?
6. Does he telegraph his passes?
7. Is he an aggressive rebounder?
8. Is he a leaper?
9. Can he shoot from outside?

10. Does he perform any role consistently in the team offense?
11. Is he a good foul shooter?
12. Does he move well without the ball?
13. Does he go to a specific area on the court each time his team has the ball?
14. Can he be overplayed?
15. Can you steal the ball from him?
16. Does he turn his back to the defense while dribbling?
17. Is he a "gunner"?
18. Does he look to hand off whenever a teammate is open?

All of these factors help to provide a fairly good picture of the offensive ability of each player.

The scout is also interested in the strategy of the *rival coach*. He should note the coach's reaction to the various game situations. For instance:

1. How does he react when his team falls behind? Will he take drastic measures immediately or will he try to work his way out of the hole?
2. Is he a coach who varies his defense from game to game or does he stick to the same defensive alignment throughout a season?
3. Will the coach attempt to have his players "match-up" with the opponents from the zone?
4. Does he substitute frequently or rarely? Can he be fooled by "match-up" defenses? Are his teams traditionally susceptible to the press?

Using the information. As indicated in an earlier section, once this information has been obtained it is carefully digested by the coaches and players, and battle plans are made. Practices are keyed toward the next game. Any newspaper clippings or magazine articles about the opponent are posted in the dressing room. Placards with watchwords such as "Stop Smith," or "Press the Titans," or "Fast-Break the Buffaloes" are also prominently displayed in the dressing room. If a team respects the opponent and thinks about the coming game, they will be psychologically "up" for the contest. It is the coach's job to generate this kind of interest. If a team takes an opponent for granted, it is susceptible to an upset. A coach must strive to have his team honed to a top psychological pitch for each game of the season. This is an extremely difficult task and hardly possible when the schedule runs 26 or more games. However, it is the coach's responsibility to do everything in his power to bring the squad to this desired level of enthusiasm.

Practice prior to the game. The last practice which a squad has before its game should be brief but meaningful. The coach goes over the important aspects of offense and defense with the squad on the floor. They should run just enough to "get a sweat up." If things are not progressing as planned, it is better to cut practice short rather than drag it out with a tedious session. As long as the players know what they have to do and have done it before, the chances are they will respond favorably to the game situation. Endless repetition of maneuvers at this time can backfire on the coach by resulting in a shoddy game performance.

Day of the game. During the day of the game the players should carry out as normal a routine as possible. Since the afternoon is free, the players should nap for a half-hour to a full hour. They should eat the pre-game meal about four hours before game time. This meal should follow the regular diet of the player. There is no real necessity for the player eating the traditional training meal of steak, baked potato, green vegetables, tea and toast with honey. This is certainly *not an undesirable* pre-game meal. In fact, this is the meal most of the St. Joseph's players take. However, some do not want such a heavy meal. Others do not like the beef or baked potato. I have found that these players perform better by eating the normal meal. They are permitted to do this as long as they adhere to the basic diet regulations.

Reliable drug firms are producing nutritive drinks which can be used in place of the pre-game meal. These products provide a favorably balanced supply of carbohydrates, proteins, fats, vitamins, and minerals in easily digested form. Such liquids have proved to be excellent for the player with the "nervous stomach" who has difficulty digesting a pre-game meal.

Coaches can experiment with this solid food substitute at evening practices and scrimmages before using it in the game situation.

Pre-game talk. Players should arrive at the game site one hour before game time. This one-hour period will enable them to dress at a leisurely pace and to have their training needs cared for before going briefly over the game plan with the coach. If the coach has "reached" his players during the preparation period of the previous days and has aroused their enthusiasm, there is no need for the traditional pep talk in the locker room prior to the game. The squad will respond to the game situation without it. Ranting and raving by the coach often tends to increase the tension which already exists and may tighten the players emotionally.

The pre-game talk is the time for individual reminders on offense and defense, and for a general resumé of the plans for the game. It is useless to go into great detail, with complex instructions. The players will not respond. They are anxious to get out on the court. The coach should give a last word of encouragement, challenge, or warning (whichever seems most appropriate) and then send them to the court.

Coach's preparation. Prior to game time, the coach should have decided how he plans to use his personnel. He should have in mind the order of substitutes, by position, in back of the starting five. He should have in mind defensive adjustments that may have to be made. The coach can profit by watching the opponents carefully as they warm up—looking for little things he may have overlooked if he saw his opponent play before or to familiarize himself with their personnel, if he is using a scouting report from someone else.

If the coach has done all these things, then both he and his team are ready to play the game.

CHAPTER 16

Coaching the Game

Although thorough pre-game preparation is vital for the successful basketball team, the coach must also be prepared to handle his team *during the game* so that the necessary offensive, defensive, and personnel adjustments are made at the appropriate time. The good coach is a meticulous, discerning observer of the game. He is sensitive to any defensive change or weakness of the opponent. He is cognizant of the effectiveness of his own defense. He is conscious of the offensive and defensive performance of each of his players and is ready to make changes in the lineup when they become necessary. The good coach is "on top" of every game situation and has an answer in reserve for each problem that presents itself. This kind of coach inspires the confidence of the team.

THE STARTING LINEUP

Use of personnel. Many coaches like to determine their five best players as early in the season as possible. This is their starting team. These are the players who will see all the action. The rest of the squad resigns itself to a season of watching and hoping next season will be different.

I have found that many advantages accrue from selecting a starting lineup according to particular game strategy. Before selecting the starting five for a game, I consider the strengths and weaknesses of the opponent. Then I weigh the merits of the players on my squad in an effort to use the best possible combination in that particular game. I will vary our starting lineup for one or several of the following:

1. To allow a big man to control the opening tap.
2. To include a defensive specialist against an opponent's high scorer.
3. To load the lineup with our best pressing combination.
4. To include a good shooter against a tough zone defense.
5. To include a good ball-handler against a possible pressing defense.
6. To offset an opponent's over-all speed advantage.
7. To offset an opponent's height advantage.
8. To include a good driver against a vulnerable man-to-man defense.
9. To overcome a "small" opponent with as much height as possible.
10. To ease a young player into the game situation.
11. To replace a "nervous starter" by opening with another player.
12. To save a consistent "foul-out" from early violations.
13. To coach the team "quarterback" on special tactics while both the coach and player can observe the opening minutes of the game from the bench.

Benefits of the varied lineup. By varying the starting lineup according to the opponent's strengths and weaknesses, the coach is sending his strongest possible team on the court at the start of each game. This maneuver may provide an early game advantage that is the final margin of victory.

This practice results in many different starting lineups during the season. I find this to be an advantage in itself. When this condition exists, there is no actual "starting team"; there is, instead, a real "team squad." Every player is a part of the team and actually contributes to the team effort. Good team morale results from this situation which permeates the entire scene—at practice, around the campus, and on trips as well as during the game.

This policy serves to keep those who start a particular game on their toes, because they know a replacement is waiting. This tends to evoke an all-out, hustling performance from each player.

Another advantage of this system is that each player on the squad gradually becomes inured to the pressures of playing and can be relied upon to enter any game situation and give a poised performance. This gives a team depth which might otherwise be lacking.

THE OPPONENT

Team defense. When the game starts, the coach's first obligation is to determine the defense which the opponent is playing. He must determine—the first time his team has possession of the ball—whether the opponent is playing man-to-man, zone, or a combination defense. The easiest way to determine this is to send one of the back-court men cutting through the lane and out to one corner or the other. It may be necessary to carry out two or three consecutive moves of this kind before the coach is sure of the defense his team is facing. If the opponent allows the cutters to go through without defensive adjustment, then the coach can be reasonably certain that the opponent is playing a standard zone. If the opponent follows each man through and checks him as he moves into his next position, then the coach knows he is faced with a straight man-to-man defense. If, on the other hand, there is internal defensive adjustment as the cutters go through, the coach knows he is being played a combination defense. The coach should have his team schooled in making an appropriate offensive response to the opponent's defense.

Even though the coach may determine what the opponent is playing defensively at the beginning of the game, he must be constantly on the alert to spot any team defensive changes. Some teams will start off in a straight zone defense, but then, after several offensive series by their opponent, will move into a combination defense. Other teams will start in a combination and then move into a straight zone. Still others will change on signals from the bench or will change after every field goal. The coach must have his team ready for these changes and make the appropriate offensive adjustments.

Team offense. The next aspect of the game for the coach to analyze is the opponent's offense. Most teams will have a planned attack. If the coach has scouted the opponent well, he will have anticipated this attack. If the offense is different than expected, it might cause him to make an immediate defensive adjustment. If the offense is what the coach expected, he must observe the game carefully in order to determine the effectiveness of his defense.

The coach must also analyze the opponent's offense as rapidly as possible to determine their offensive objectives. He must discern the type game the opponent wants to play. Is he attempting to play a deliberate game? Does he want to fast-break? Is he running a pattern style of offense? Is he using a set play type of game? Once the coach has determined the offensive objectives of the opponent, then he is better able to make whatever defensive adjustments may be necessary to contain his offensive attack.

Individuals. Once the opponent's team offensive and defensive efforts have been analyzed, the coach turns his attention to the individual players. Since we do a lot of pressing, I am especially concerned with the ball-handling ability of these individuals. Of special importance is the ball-handling ability of the back-court men. Having previously made a judgment on this ability while scouting, I am anxious to see how the guards actually handle the ball against our pressing defense. I note carefully how poised they are in advancing the ball and how well they dribble and pass against the harassing tactics of our defensive men. Then I look for these specific items:

1. Do the back-court men look for the outlet pass to the high post-man?
2. Does the high post-man come to meet the ball?
3. Do post-men take position in the middle of the court or at the side area?
4. Which players can we really overplay?
5. Which players turn their backs to the defense with or without the ball?
6. On which players can we successfully double-up?
7. Which players seem to be having an especially good shooting night?
8. Must we overplay them more to keep them from receiving a pass?
9. Which players are rebounding aggressively?
10. Are the rebounders "jumping over" our defensive men?
11. Is a substitution necessary to combat any of these advantages of the opponent?
12. Which of the opponents seem to be tiring?
13. Which of them offers the greatest defensive weakness on which we might capitalize?
14. Which player is slow in getting back on defense?
15. Is one of the opponents susceptible to a one-on-one driving situation caused either by poor defensive ability or personal foul trouble?

The coach makes these observations as early as possible in the ball game. These judgments and decisions will help provide him with a backlog of reference to which he may refer in planning later offensive and defensive strategy.

YOUR TEAM

Team defense. After the coach has given a quick analysis of the opponent's offense, defense, and individual play, he turns his attention to his own team. Of prime consideration is his team defense:

1. Is the planned defense doing the job the coach expected it to do?
2. If it is not, is it the fault of the defense itself?
3. Does the opponent's attack necessitate a change in the point at which the defense is applied?
4. Does the opponent's attack necessitate a change in the defensive structure?
5. Is the opponent consistently exploiting a defensive weakness which can be adjusted?

Team offense. Considering his team's offensive work, the coach must quickly supply answers to the following questions:

1. Are we getting the kind of shots we had planned?
2. Is the opponent thwarting our offensive efforts by a particular defensive move?
3. Does the opponent's defense necessitate a change in the objectives or in the mode of our attack?
4. Are we getting "inside" the opponent's defense with the offense?
5. Are we forced to shoot from around the perimeter of the opponent's defense?
6. Are we in position to rebound aggressively off the offensive board?
7. Is there a weakness in the opponent's defense which we may exploit as a team?

INDIVIDUALS

Once the team situation has been sized up then the coach turns his attention to the individual play of his team members. In our pressing game, we are concerned with the individual player's ability to contribute to the planned offensive and defensive attack.

Defense

1. *Is each player* doing an effective job of stopping the dribbler?
2. *Is he* effectively overplaying the outlet pass receiver?
3. *Is he* effectively sloughing off his man to jam the cutting and passing lanes?
4. *Is he* effectively blocking out under the defensive backboard?
5. Is a substitution necessary to overcome any defect in the execution of the above?
6. Does the opponent present an individual or an attack that is too much for any squad member to cope with under the existing alignment?

Offense

1. *Is each player* contributing to the effectiveness of the planned offense?
2. *Is each* working with the others to achieve team performance?
3. *Is each* capable of getting the good shot from the planned offensive attack?
4. *Is each* rebounding as expected or is he letting himself get screened out?
5. Do some players appear to be tiring?
6. Do some players seem to be having an "off night"?
7. Is one of the opponent's defensive players able to stymie the offensive efforts of your own player?
8. Is the opponent's defensive structure halting the offensive play of one or more of your players?

SUBSTITUTING

Some coaches are very reluctant to go to the bench at any time in the game. Some coaches will use five men for as much of a ball game as is possible. I feel that if a player is worth carrying on the squad then he should be able to help the team. By carrying a light squad (usually 10 players), I find that each player can be given the opportunity to contribute to the success of the team. The value of this policy has been stated in the section concerning the selection of the starting lineup.

When to substitute:

1. *Substitute early in the ball game.* Try to get each player, who is likely to play in the game at all, into the contest during the first half. This enables him to get the feel of the game and to reduce tension. Then if he has to come back in the game at a crucial point in the second half, he is ready. I have found it to be good policy to substitute sophomore players early in the game so that they may accumulate experience at a time when the possible damage to your team is less serious.

2. *Substitute for a tired or injured player.* A player who is excessively tired or injured is of limited value to the team. The coach is better off to substitute a player of lesser ability than to stay with one who cannot give his full worth to the team.

3. *Substitute for a player or players when the game is not going as planned.* If your team has fallen behind in the game then some change is necessary. It may be a change in defense or it may be a change in personnel. Sometimes, regardless of the defensive or offensive changes which the coach initiates, the trend in the game does not change. Then it becomes necessary to change the personnel.

4. *Substitute for players who are not contributing enough to the offense or who are not strong enough defensively.*

5. *Substitute players of like abilities.* Back-court men are substituted for back-court men, forwards for forwards, centers for centers. Make certain that the substitute can do the offensive and defensive job called for in the ball game at that particular moment.

6. *Substitute to obtain special skills.* There may be occasion when the coach finds it necessary to substitute players skilled in a particular phase of the game. For example, it might be necessary at a point in the game to get as much defensive speed in the lineup for a pressing formation. Or, the coach might want his best foul shooters and ball-handlers in the lineup when he has taken a lead at the end of a game. In this manner he can maintain his lead with good ball-handling and, at the same time, have good pressure foul shooters available if the opponent fouls in his attempts to get the ball.

7. *Substitute to get a strong defensive man in the lineup.* If one of the opposition is consistently hurting your team by scoring, rebounding, or ball-handling, there may be someone on the bench who can nullify these efforts.

8. *Substitute to get a particular offensive skill in the lineup.*
   a. Insert a jump shooter into your lineup to cope with a particular type of zone opening.
   b. Add more height to your team if it is being consistently out-rebounded.
   c. Get better ball-handlers into the lineup if your team is having difficulty with a pressing defense.
   d. Substitute a tall player at a jump ball situation so that your team will have a big target to which to tap the ball.
   e. Substitute tall players on a crucial foul shot so that if it is missed the big man will be in position to get the rebound.*

9. *Substitute for a player having a bad night.* Sometimes brief periods of rest will enable a player to re-enter the game and reach a higher level of performance than he demonstrated earlier. This is often true of the high scorer in a big game who feels that he must carry his team to victory. Sometimes these players, overridden with tension, require brief periods on the bench to maintain top level efficiency.

THE TIME-OUT

College teams are allowed five one-minute time-out periods during the regulation game and one additional for each overtime period. The coach should use these cautiously. He should try to conserve his times out for the occasions when they are really needed. The time-out is a strategic move rather than a rest period. It is a time to influence the course of the game.

I save two for an end-of-game situation if at all possible. This leaves us only three times-out for the first half and most of the second half. Since these periods are at a premium, I try to do the work usually reserved for time-out periods while the actual game is in progress. Therefore, when a player is shooting a foul for either team, I like to have my back-court leader come over for a conference so that he may relay any minor adjustments to the other players—either to the offense or the defense. A coach also has an opportunity to relay instructions to his players when his team is advancing the ball up-court to offensive positions. In this situation it is extremely helpful for the coach to have visual signals by which he can pass information to his floor leader.

Radical change. To effect radical changes in offense or defense,

---

* Players inserted for these latter special tactics can be removed from the lineup immediately following the play. As soon as possession is obtained your team can call time-out and the coach can re-align his forces.

however, it is well for the coach to take the time-out. Major changes in play must be clearly understood by all players. If they are not understood, the situation may go from bad to worse. Such a change in either aspect of the game may become necessary if the opponent has found a weakness which he is exploiting.

Opponent's hot streak. Another occasion for the time-out occurs when the opponent has run off an uninterrupted streak of points. The alert coach anticipates such a series and nips it, before it changes the complexion of the game, with a time-out and perhaps some adjustment to the offense or the defense.

Fatigue. Times-out may also be taken if a player or players on the team are overly fatigued. For the most part, however, it is better to substitute for such a player and give him a rest on the bench rather than take the time-out.

The double time-out. It is sometimes strategically profitable to take times-out back to back. The situation might arise at an especially critical part of the game in which it is necessary for the players to understand exactly what is expected of them. If the coach has saved his times-out, he has double the time to get the information across clearly to his players.

It may also seem beneficial to use this measure at the end of a keenly contested game, in order to give the players the benefit of a double rest period.

Player in dangerous situation. It is advisable for players to call time-out if they are stuck with the ball in a poor passing position. It is better that the man take time-out than take a chance in throwing a bad pass.

Consultation with officials. It may be necessary sometimes for the coach to take a time-out in order to consult with the referee on a particular ruling or judgment. This should be used rarely, but if there seems to be a conflict of understanding concerning the rules or the procedure of the game, such a time-out may be very well spent.

Conducting the time-out. The coach has one minute to give instructions to his team during the time-out. The instructions must be clear and concise—providing general information for the team and brief specific directions to the individuals.

In order to hold the attention of his players, the coach should face them as they sit on the bench with the rest of the squad grouped about to hear what is being said. The managers and trainer can care for the physical needs of the players while the coach is at work.

Although the coach conducts the time-out, he should be willing to listen to a player who feels he has something valuable to contribute to the brief meeting.

HALF TIME

College teams have 15 minutes between halves of the game. The first few minutes of this period should be reserved for relaxation and rest. This time may also be used for the trainer to check injuries or possible discomforts of the players. Cokes and orange segments may be provided.

Since the coach will want to allow a few minutes for the players to warm up briefly before the beginning of the second half, there is about 10 minutes to go over the progress of the game; make any changes in offense, defense, or personnel, and "fire up" the team for the all-important half.

The procedure during this period depends on how the game has progressed. If the coach feels that his team has not been playing up to capacity, a spirited talk may be of great value during the first part of this period. It is a time when players can be roused from their lethargy and spurred on to greater efforts in the second half. After this "pep talk," the coach should finish with a definite plan for a renewed and vigorous offensive and defense in the second half. He should indicate lineup changes so that players who are going to start the second half will know exactly what is expected of them.

If, on the other hand, the team has played well in the first half, it is better to go over the plans for second half activities first—including possible alterations in offensive or defensive tactics and lineup changes. Then, just before the team leaves the dressing room to warm up for the second half, the coach should rally them together with a few words of warning and encouragement so that the first half's advantage doesn't slip away. Teams should be allowed at least three minutes to prepare for the second half. This is especially true if there are lineup changes and players who have not been playing a great deal are going to start the second half.

END OF THE GAME

It is often said that the coach proves his merit in the final minutes of the game. If his team is ahead, it is up to the coach to maintain that lead until the final buzzer. If his team is behind, then it is up to the coach to do all in his power to overcome the deficit.

Team ahead. If one's team is ahead going into the closing minutes of the game, it is well to remember two things. First, the team obtained its lead by attacking the opponent's defense. If the coach expects to retain the lead he must constantly threaten the attack for the scoring play and, if the defense permits, take advantage of defensive lapses to increase his advantage. I have seen a great many games lost by teams which stifled their attack too early in the game and ran out of momentum when they found it necessary to renew their attempts to score. If a team is satisfied with its lead and isn't looking for opportunities to add to such a lead, the defensive team may increase its chances to obtain possession of the ball. There is also a psychological factor involved here that is very important. The team that has stopped its attempts to score will find it difficult to regain the aggressive edge necessary to win the close ones.

The team that is constantly seeking to add to its advantage is a tough team to counter at the end of the game. Consequently, when my team is ahead, I want it always to look for opportunities to increase its lead. Whether it comes on the drive for the basket, a pass for a short lay-up or short jump shot, or by forcing the opponent to foul one of our players in control of the ball, we are trying to add to our advantage. We are striving to maintain offensive pressure on our opponent right up to the end of the game.

Team behind. When the coach finds his team trailing in the closing minutes of the game, he must do something about the situation. He must use defensive tactics that will obtain quick possession of the ball. This situation demands some kind of a pressing defense. The defensive team must take chances—more chances than they normally would to obtain possession. Once it has obtained possession, it must attack quickly to obtain a good shot. The amount of time taken to set up this good shot depends upon the amount of the deficit and the amount of time remaining in the game. If there is very little time—six points down with a minute and a half to play—then the team must attack and get the quick shot as soon as it can get the ball over mid-court and work into shooting position.

If, on the other hand, the team is one point behind and a minute and a half to play, it may work carefully to get that good shot. As soon as it gets the good shot, it should take advantage of the opportunity. It is better to put the pressure on the opponent in such a situation by scoring at the first opportunity, than to wait for a final shot just before the end of the game. In such a circumstance, the team may not succeed in its attempts and will thereby lose the game. I would rather gain the lead and then put the pressure on the opponent to do something about the situation.

Tie score. If the score is tied near the end of the game, and his team has the ball, the coach must decide whether to go for the field goal immediately or whether to hold the ball and try for one shot. Much depends on the defensive tactics of the opponent. If the defense is going to lay back and wait, then I would prefer to hold the ball and get the last second shot. This shot should come from a planned play with several options so that if the originally intended play does not succeed, there will be other opportunities to score.

If, however, the opponent is going to press and take an all-out gamble on obtaining possession of the ball before we can set up a last-minute play, I want my team to take advantage of any defensive lapse so we may get the short high percentage shot. If we are successful in obtaining the lead at this time, we want to pressure our opponent to make him consume as much time as possible in advancing the ball to shooting position. We are careful not to be drawn into a foul situation, but we are putting as much pressure as we safely can on the opponent. Never give him an uncontested shot when a field goal can tie or win for the opponent.

If the score is tied and the opponent has the ball at the end of the game, the coach should effect an unexpected defensive change to keep the opponent off balance and obtain possession of the ball. It has been indicated in earlier chapters how the straight zone and zone press defenses may be used on such occasions. The coach must make any lineup changes necessary to have his strongest defensive force at work in this situation. If his defensive tactics work favorably, his team can take time out so the best offensive players can be inserted for the final effort to score.

The important factor is to prevent the opponent from carrying out his scoring objective. If he does this, he wins the game. Unexpected defensive change is the *answer*.

CHAPTER 17

Tournament
Play

For most high school and college teams the culmination of the season's work is participation in a post-season tournament. Each season at St. Joseph's College, we set as our objective the participation in one of the national tournaments. In order to participate in the National Collegiate Athletic Association (N.C.A.A.) tournament, we know we must win the Middle Atlantic Conference Championship. If we should fail in that objective, we know we must have a fine record in order to be selected for the National Invitational Tournament (N.I.T.). These objectives are constantly before us. It helps to make each game important for us.

TOURNAMENT PRACTICE

If we succeed in making a tournament, then we want to do as well as we possibly can. Success depends a great deal on proper planning. The problems of practicing for tournament play are the same at any level of competition. There is always the problem of spacing the practice sessions after the completion of the last regularly scheduled game of the season and before the first tournament game. If the lay-off is a week or more, the coach may feel it advisable to give several days off before regrouping the squad for practice for the first tournament game. The coach is guided by his awareness of the mental and physical condition of the team. The basketball season is a long one. The coach may feel that the best preparation for the tournament is several days off for his squad. Whatever his policy, he should have definite team plans made when the squad reconvenes. If possible, he should have seen his opponent play. It is advantageous to have seen the opponent play as near to tournament time as possible. With this report before him (whether obtained by himself or someone in whom he has complete confidence), the coach makes his plan for the first tournament game.

The game plan. The coach should not depart too radically from the plan of attack his team used during the regular season. After all, he got to the tournament by playing as he did in the regular season. If it was good enough to get him to the tournament, it may well be good enough to get him through it. Therefore, the coach's plan will be based on the same careful analysis of the opponent as was made during the season.

Travel to tournament site. If the site of the tournament is more than 100 miles away, the coach should plan to arrive the day before the game. He should check accommodations for his squad to make certain that there are proper eating and resting facilities. The coach should schedule a workout at the site of the tournament on the day of his arrival. At the workout, he should emphasize shooting and ball-handling, using full-court drills so the players will get the feel of the floor and the positions of the baskets. It is helpful for the team to return to the court for a brief shooting workout the day of the tournament. This second exposure to the floor often provides a better familiarity with the surroundings. This, in turn, may lead to a good shooting night.

If the competing team is from a location relatively close to the tournament site, then the coach plans to take his team to the game site on the day of the game. He should arrive early enough to allow his team to get a short shooting period on the floor prior to game time. If the team is at the tournament site for an extended period of time (more than two hours before game time) the coach should see to it that the players have accommodations for lying down and resting prior to the game.

Some of the best tournament performances of teams I have coached have followed morning workouts on the day of the game. Very often this kind of activity is better for the players than sitting around in a hotel room or wandering the streets while building up nervous tension.

Meals and rest period. Once again the routine for tournament play should follow that established during the regular season. If the coach has had his team rise at a definite hour when playing away games, he should continue this policy. If the coach has not insisted on this, there is no need for establishing a different policy at this time of the year. The same procedure should be followed in the time set for meals and the meal menu. Players relax much more if they are following a routine to which they are accustomed.

Pre-game meeting. It seems unlikely that the coach will have to use any ruse to arouse the enthusiasm of his team for tournament play. Players who have strived all season to participate in the tournament will hardly need any encouragement to get out and play the best basketball they know how. On the contrary, the coach may very well settle his team down by bringing a little levity into the locker room. This helps to dispel the tension almost certain to exist.

The tournament outcome. The winning of a post-season tournament is the ultimate objective of all coaches. It is a great objective for which to strive. Few actually achieve it at the college level. Therefore, the coach should look upon participation in the post-season tournament as reward enough and should derive satisfaction from this. By participating frequently in the tournaments, he enhances his chances of going all the way to win the big one.

CHAPTER 18

Post-Game
Relationships

When the game is over the coach is expected to perform in the manner of the school's official representative—whether his team has won or lost. He is expected to display the highest level of sportsmanship. The team he coaches is expected to perform in a similar manner. This is an exceptionally difficult task. It is difficult to restrain one's exuberance when he has achieved a goal for which he has worked hard, possibly for weeks and months. It is equally difficult to conceal a chagrin which one feels after planning, working, and praying for the attainment of an objective which has been denied him. This is one of the lessons in life imparted through competition and athletics. The coach and players must learn to accept victory and defeat with as nearly equal grace as possible.

The opponent. If the opponent has won the game, congratulations should be extended to them by the losing coach and his players. This is an obligation which comes with losing. Offering congratulations may be the last thing in the world that the coach and players feel like doing at the moment. However, another lesson applicable in life is learned through this act. It teaches humility and, more than that, manifests the fact that not all worthy and hard-fought-for goals are reached. It teaches that sometimes no matter how hard one has worked and how nobly one has played, the prize will still be denied him.

For the victorious coach, there is a great feeling of satisfaction that comes from attaining a realistic objective. He must, however, learn to contain his feelings of euphoria when chatting with the losing coach. He must remember how narrow is the margin of victory and remember his own feelings in defeat. Losing coaches are rarely talkative. A few brief words to the losing coach and wishes for success in the remainder of the season are about as much as the winning coach should wish to impose on the loser.

The winning coach should avoid trips to the losing team's locker room even if the intention is to extend congratulations on a well-played game. The losing team is not in the mood to receive such visits. This commendable wish can be expressed by mail and will reach the losing coach at a time when he is more willing to appreciate the message.

Own players. The coach should be available to his players after the game unless there are extenuating circumstances which prevent this. The coach should remain in the locker room until all the players have dressed and have left the room. If his team has played well—whether they've won or lost—the coach should congratulate the players on their performance. In winning the big games the coach may well temper his praise with the knowledge that there are usually many tough games lying ahead of the team and complacency is something to be avoided like the plague. That does *not* mean that he cannot join in the festivities that follow the winning of such a contest. This is one of the joys of coaching. It *does* mean that he must keep his players at an approachable level so that no matter how well the team has played, he is still the coach and they are willing to listen to him.

The team that has played well and lost needs all the morale boosting that a coach can give it. Defeat is not something that can be shrugged off with casual reflection. However, the coach cannot have his team brooding over a defeat. There are too many games in the season for that. The recuperative power of a successful basketball team must be rapid. They must be able to take defeat, realize its seriousness, make whatever adjustments are necessary, and come back strong a few nights later in another contest.

If a team has given an unimpressive or shoddy performance, whether it has won or lost, it should be made aware of the coach's dissatisfaction. This should not take the form of a lengthy post-game harangue or extended analysis of the game. The time for that (if necessary at all) is prior to the next practice session. By the same token, however, the team expects something from the coach on such occasions. Usually a brief but pointed criticism will serve the purpose.

If the coach feels that the squad should be taken to task for an inept performance, he should go about it in a thorough manner so that the players know just how the coach feels about the situation. A team meeting prior to the next practice provides a suitable climate for this session. Very often it may be necessary to "clear the air" after a performance of this kind. It may be that there is dissension among the players. Perhaps there is dissatisfaction with the way the coach is running things. There may be any number of other factors. These cannot be ignored. They are best brought into the open, considered objectively, and attempts made to reach a logical solution.

Sometimes private conferences with individual players are necessary. Such conferences often reveal situations of which the coach had no knowledge. Such meetings can be invaluable in settling difficulties that exist among squad members.

The coach's principal job after a defeat is to rally the team. He must help them to set their collective sights on the objective of winning the next game. He must obtain the full cooperation of everyone connected with the team.

Don't adopt a "You can't win them all" philosophy. It has been proven that *you can* win them all. The team that feels that it can't, won't. The team that feels that it can win them all, may very well do just that. The coach has a great deal to do with the acceptance of such philosophies. He must be a leader. He must be enthusiastic and confident, while realizing what it takes to accomplish the objectives which he has before him.

The press. The newspaper is the medium by which most sports fans learn the particulars about an athletic contest. Basketball games are no exception. One of the techniques used by newspapermen to uncover the technicalities of the completed game is to interview the coach. The coach should be willing to grant the interview and provide the requested information. He should, however, learn to choose his words carefully so that they convey the exact meaning intended. Quotations have a habit of taking on a somewhat different meaning when they appear in print—although this is not necessarily the fault of the writer.

If his team has won the game, the coach will find the post-game interview easily carried off. Most coaches have little difficulty in finding words of praise for the members of their team and the opponent after a victorious game. A far more difficult time is after a defeat. The members of the press are often interested in finding out the coach's views on why the team lost. The coach should be as objective as possible. He should not enter into personalities. He should not place the blame on a particular player nor should he publicly accept the blame himself—even though he may feel this burden. Self-criticism by the coach shakes squad morale. It won't take much of the "It was my fault" explanation by the coach before the players, school officials, and public will believe him. Comments about a defeat should pertain to team performance. Outstanding individual performances by members of either team, the ability of the opponent, general shortcomings of one's team—are topics which will help the losing coach get past this situation.

The coach can help himself, his team, and the institution he represents by establishing these three regulations for post-game interviews.

1. Give the team about 10 minutes in the locker room before any member of the press is admitted.
2. Request that the press ask the coach's permission before interviewing a player.
3. Request that the press refrain from interviewing the coach or players on the same day of a defeat.

The press can be of great assistance to the coach and to the promotion of basketball. The vast majority of the writers whom I have known have been sincere, dedicated men who are interested in doing all they can to advance the cause of competitive athletics. The coach owes these men the obligation of providing as much accurate information as he can. The above suggestions are made with the intention of improving the relations between the coach and the press.

The spectator. The coach must realize that the spectator's attitude toward the game is usually far different than his own. For the spectator, the game is entertainment and affords him an opportunity to go out and root for his favorite team and against the opponent. From my experience there is developing an increasing number of well-behaved sportsmen who follow collegiate basketball. These are the spectators who applaud a good play regardless of who performs it. They accept the officials' decision without loud protestation. They will treat the visiting team and its followers as guests. It is a pleasure to play before such spectators.

There is also a minority element which cannot be classified as good sportsmen. These are the hooters, the booers, the jeerers and, in some instances, the rioters. These are the people who come to games for the expressed purpose of hurling derisive remarks at the opposing spectators, players, and coach. The coach must develop a thick skin which is impervious to the barbs of such spectators. He can't let himself be lured into verbal combat with such people. It will detract from the quality of his coaching. He has too many important things to do than to bother with this type of person. There are times when this is a difficult thing to do. However, the "loud-mouth" is best ignored.

Summary. The basketball coach is in a unique position. He works through a long season in which his team may play as many as thirty games.

He must be an expert public relations man to deal with the rabid spectators jammed in about him. He must have the patience of Job. He must struggle to attain something that is sometimes near impossible. If he doesn't attain it, he is expected to smile graciously, congratulate his adversary, and pick up immediately to set out for new goals.

If the coach does attain his objective, he is expected to conceal his exuberance and enthusiasm and accept the well wishes of those who really expected it of him all the time. Then he must maintain a level-headed team attitude necessary for taking on the next opponent a few nights later. Coaching is the only occupation where thousands of individuals—many "experts"—look over your shoulder while you are working and offer a variety of suggestions on how to get the job done.

And yet, for all this, there is an army of dedicated men throughout the nation (at college, high school, elementary school, and independent levels) who truly love coaching. I have found personal inspiration from contacts with these men at coaching clinics. The enthusiasm they display in their quest for general information about the game and on the techniques of teaching fundamental skills is boundless. These are the coaches who are seeking improved methods of developing individuals into better team units.

These men are seeking the real reward of coaching. They find satisfaction in individual and team development on the court. They take pride in seeing the boys they coach develop into better citizens because of their participation in basketball. They are able to share with their players the sweet taste of victory and the bitter dregs of defeat. It is a communion which no other walk of life permits.

Index

Advancing the ball, fast break, 153
Analysis of opponent
   during the game
      checking the opponent, 205-
         206
      own team, 207-208
   scouting
      coach, 199
      individual, 198-199
      team, 197-198
Ankle injuries, 194-195
Attack
   fast-break, 151-155
   freeze, 171-174
   man-to-man, 155-163
   press, 167-171
   zone, 163-166

Ball handling, 110-122
Baseball pass, 112
Bevans, Rollie, 194
   (*Athletic Trainers' Handbook*)
Body balance, defense, 7-11
Bounce pass, 111
Boxer's glide step, 9-11

Calculated risk, 45

Center
   defensive play, 73, 74
   offensive play, 107, 155-166
Change-of-direction dribble, 114
Change-of-direction moves, 143
Change-of-pace dribble, 114
Chest pass, 110
Citizenship, democratic objectives for
   players, viii
Clearing a side, 161-162
Coaching during the game, 203-214
Coaching during the half, 212
Coaching at time-out, 211
Concentration, lay-up shooting, 125
Conditioning, 188-189
Control of game by pressing defense,
   79-83
Cramer Chemical Company, 194
   Helpful Hints from the First
      Aider
Cross-over step, 118-119
Cutting the squad, 187-188

Defense
   defensive thinking, 3
   practice time allotted to, 4
   special skills, 15-22

Defense (*cont.*):
   strategic use of, 79-86
   team defenses, 29-102
Defense, pressing
   basic principles, 11-15
   defensive flick, 21-24
   double-up, 18-21, 40-42
   faking, 15-17
   flexibility of, 45
   individual drills, 24-26
   movement, 9-11
   objectives, 4
   playing man with ball, 11-12
   playing man without ball, 13-14
   rebounding, 14-15, 42-43
   strategic use, 79-83
Defensive shuffle, 9-11
Diet, 195-196
Dribbling,
   change-of-direction, 114
   change-of-pace, 114
   control dribble, 114
   drills, 145-147
   reverse dribble, 116
   speed dribble, 114
   spin dribble, 116
   switch dribble, 114
Drinking, problem of, 196
Driving
   cross-over, 118-119
   drills, 116
   rocker step, 120-122
   techniques, 116-122

Exercises
   isometric, 192
   isotonic, 191

Facing the ball on defense, 13-14
Fast-break offense,
   drill, 154
   three-lane attack, 151-155
Ferguson, William J., vii
Finger signals, 80
Fingers, use of,
   dribbling, 114

Fingers, use of (*cont.*):
   passing, 110
   shooting, 129
Flexibility of defense, 45
Foot position, defense, 7-9
Foot moves, offense, 118-122
Forwards
   defensive play, 72-74
   offensive play, 107-108, 151-166
Free throw shooting, 135-138
Freeze offense
   man-to-man, 172-173
   zone, 174

Game preparation, 84-88, 166-169
   scouting, 197-199
   the starting lineup, 203-205
Guards,
   defensive play, 72, 73
   offensive play, 155-166
Guards, characteristics, 72-73

Hands
   use of in dribbling, 113-117
   use of in passing, 110
Hedging, 37-38
Hoffman, Bob, 190
Hook pass, 112

Injuries, 194-195
Isometric contraction exercise
   definition, 189
   equipment, 194
   experimentation, 189-192
   program, 192
Isotonic contraction exercise
   definition, 189
   overload theory, 191

Jump ball formations, 176-179
Jump ball, use of signals, 176
Jumping increase in ability, 189-191
Jump switch, 36-37

Knees, flexed position, 7

Lay-up shooting
concentration in, 125
technique, 123-125
Locker room
signs, 199
talks, 200
Low post attack, 162-163

Man-to-man team defense
flexibility of, 45
rules of operation, 30
rules of operation, application of,
32-44
Man-to-man team offense, 155-166
fast break, 151-155
freeze, 172-173
high post attack, 155-162
low post attack, 162-163
Meals on trips, 195-196, 200
Medicine balls, use in practice, 191

Nutrition drinks, 200

Offense
against the press, 167-171
fast break, 151-155
freeze, 171-174
man-to-man, 155-163
one-on-one
clear-out, 161-162
skills, 116-122
out-of-bounds plays, 180-184
stall, 171
use of material, 106-108
zone offense, 163-166
Offense, relationship to defense, 105-
108
Offensive drills, 139-149
Offensive skills,
dribbling, 113-116
passing, 110-113
shooting, 123-136

Passing
bounce pass, 111
chest pass, 110

Passing (cont.):
drills, 139-144
hand-off pass, 113
outlet pass, 112
Pass receiving, 110
Peripheral vision, use of, 7
Pettit, Bob, 190
Philosophy of coaching, vi
application of philosophy, vi-viii
coaching objectives, vi
Picking-up, 42
Pivot, foot position, 143
Possession of the ball, fast break, 151
Post-game relationships
opponent, 219
players, 220-221
press, 221-222
spectator, 222
Post play, 142, 147, 155-166
Practice sessions
game preparation, 100-101
planning of, 95-99
pre-season schedule, 96-99
Pre-game meal, 200
Pre-game talk, 200-201
Pressing defense
adjustment of available material
full-court, man-to-man,
72-73
half-court, man-to-man,
73-74
zone press, 74-76
see defense, pressing
Principles of defense, 11-15

Rebounding
defensive, 14-15, 42-43
drills, 147-148
offensive, 138-139
Rest, 196
Reverse dribble, 116

Scouting
coach, 199
individual, 198-199
team, 197-198

Shooting
    foul shooting, 135-138
    hook shot, 133-134
    jump shot, 125-130
    lay-up, 123-125
    set shot, 130-132
Sloughing off, 34-36
Smoking, problem of, 196
Special defensive skills
    defensive fake, 15-17
    defensive "flick," 21-24
    double-up, 18-21, 40-42
    double-up, conditions for, 18-21
Spectators, coach's dealings with, 222
Staleness, 188-189
Stall offense, 171
Standard zone defense
    strategic use of, 85-86
    teaching zone defense, 92-93
    1-2-2 zone defense, 86-89
    1-3-1 zone defense, 89-92
Steinhaus, Arthur, 191-192
Strategy, end of the game, 212-214
Strategic use of pressing defense, 79-83
    control tempo of game, 79
    end of the game, 80-81
    last ditch effort, 81-82
    surprise element, 80
    use of signals, 80
    when to press, 81-82
    whom to press, 83
Substitutions
    when to substitute, 209-210
Switching on defense, 36-37, 42

Tap-in, offensive, 138-139
Team defense
    man-to-man pressure, 29-46
    standard zone, 85-93
    zone press, 47-69
Team, number on, 187-188
Team offense
    against the press, 167-171
    fast break, 151-155
    freeze, 171-174
    man-to-man, 155-163
    stall, 171
    zone offense, 163-166
Time-out, 210
    strategic use of, 210-211
Tournament play
    arrangements for, 215-217
    game plan, 216
    practice, 215-216
Trainer's duties, 194-195

Underhand free throw, 136
Underhand lay-up, 124

York Barbell Company, 190

Zone offense, 163-166
Zone press,
    double-up, 48
    full-court 3-1-1, 51-52
    half-court 3-1-1, 53-55
    1-2-2 zone press, 65-69
    player responsibilities, 49
    principles of, 47
    St. Joseph's 3-1-1, 48-60
    2-2-1 zone press, 60-64